~~WELCOME~~ TO CALIFORNIA

FROM L.A. COUNTY JAIL TO #1 IN SALES

BY

SANDRA LA BOSZKO

FriesenPress

Suite 300 - 990 Fort St
Victoria, BC, V8V 3K2
Canada

www.friesenpress.com

Copyright © 2019 by Sandra LA Boszko
First Edition — 2019

Editor: Jenny Gates
Photographer: Hong Yan

All rights reserved.

No part of this publication may be reproduced in any form, or by any means, electronic or mechanical, including photocopying, recording, or any information browsing, storage, or retrieval system, without permission in writing from FriesenPress.

ISBN
978-1-5255-4643-3 (Hardcover)
978-1-5255-4644-0 (Paperback)
978-1-5255-4645-7 (eBook)

1. BIOGRAPHY & AUTOBIOGRAPHY, PERSONAL MEMOIRS

Distributed to the trade by The Ingram Book Company

Contact:
Sandra LeeAnne Boszko
sandralaboszko.com

My memoir is a true story. My parents as well as my aunt and uncle helped me with the details. Some characteristics and all names of individuals have been changed except for my brother Michael.

"Nothing is more important than

empathy

for another human being's suffering.

Not a career.

Not wealth.

Not intelligence.

Certainly not status.

We have to feel for one

another

if we're going to survive with

dignity."

-Audrey Hepburn

CHAPTER 1

Back to L.A.

Third time's a charm, right? Praying that the stars would align, I headed back to L.A. for the third time in two years to pursue my secret dream of acting.

Right before Christmas 2010, at age thirty-one, I gave my notice at Boston Pizza. A few days later, my parents and I left Winnipeg in my black two-door 1997 Sunfire with roll-up windows. That was the vehicle I would use to pursue my passion of acting. My parents were the only ones who knew acting was why I really wanted to go to L.A., and they were extremely supportive of me and more than happy to make the trip there with me. They just wished they had known about my aspirations when I was younger so they could've helped me sooner. I loved them for that.

The only thing missing on that road trip was my brother Michael. There used to be four of us on those trips, but now he was married and had his own family. When we were younger, he would sit like a guy, taking up half the back seat with his legs stretched out, and tease me about anything and everything a big brother would tease a little sister about. His arms would flip back and forth to my side of the seat as he said, "Flip, flop." He would do anything to get a reaction out of me.

Over the next four days, we travelled through eight states—North Dakota, South Dakota, Nebraska, Kansas, Oklahoma, New Mexico, Arizona, and finally Nevada. When we arrived in the town of Primm, we were disappointed to learn that snowstorms in California had forced the closure of the I-15 out of Nevada. I wanted to get to L.A. so bad, but instead I was stuck in Primm. We only had a couple of days to get to L.A. before the start of my acting classes.

Our hotel room was on the ground floor, and as soon as you walked out of it and down a long hallway, the casino was right there. To ease the stress of waiting, we shopped at the outlets during the day, and at night I played the minimum bet at the blackjack table while my parents played the slots.

When I pulled up a chair at one of the tables there was a guy sitting next to me by the name of Giovanni. He had piercing green eyes and the most perfect face. He worked in real estate. He was younger than me, but still seemed interested. We flirted and exchanged numbers, and I sensed a connection with him. At that time, I was working on feeling more and thinking less. However, when my armpits started to sweat I realized that the "feeling more, thinking less" motto could only work in terms of my acting. I briefly excused myself, went to my hotel room, quickly used the blow dryer to dry the sweat marks off my shirt, and freshened up my make-up. When I went back to the table, he was gone. I felt dejected.

Then I remembered I still had his number on a piece of paper in my hand. I hurried to the car and retrieved my Virgin mobile cards so I could connect my U.S. black plastic cell phone. I wasn't going to connect the phone until I got to L.A., but I couldn't wait any longer. I had to use it to text Giovanni right away. Because I was so excited about connecting with him, I wondered whether

I was going bipolar, but that question only lingered for a second before immediately leaving my mind.

That is exactly why I have trouble in relationships now—because I am afraid to let myself feel. My brain somehow thinks if I have feelings, I'm going to go manic—feel euphoric, have high-flown energy, have delusions, and be over-stimulated. So instead I push down my feelings and don't allow them to surface. Either that, or I remain a soloist and live my life alone, which sometimes, I have to admit, seems so much easier.

When I texted "Hi Giovanni green eyes. What are you up to?" there was no response. I was hurt, so to help me forget about the text, I tried to focus on my upcoming acting classes. The next morning, however, he and I ran into each other in the restaurant. We talked for about twenty minutes and hugged goodbye. Later that day he finally answered my text, explaining his phone had been dead. We messaged for a couple of days, but that was it.

Wednesday

After the I-15 opened, my parents and I finally hit the road. It was only a few hours to L.A., but even so, we were all relieved to get there after the unfortunate delay in our plans. The apartment I rented had a double bed and a twin bed with 1970s purple-and-pink-style bedspreads and curtains, a small dresser in the corner, an old desk, and a tiny six-square-foot old appliance kitchen cramped off to one side.

We went out shopping in the afternoon, and bought shoes from Off Broadway Shoes, a ginormous shoe store with discount name brands. I also purchased another pair of shoes, a roll of black duct tape, and a small, square, suitcase-like box with a handle from a discount store called Ross Dress for Less. I was going to use the case as a purse to carry my pen and notepad for my acting classes. My dad eventually covered that case with the black duct tape exactly the way I wanted. He helped me make it my own; he knew I often did things a little differently.

I also needed a printer to print off my acting resumes, and while I was looking for one in Target, the strangest thing happened. A guy about five feet ten smiled at me and handed me a receipt with his phone number on it. He didn't say a word. Never before had a guy passed me his number and not talked to me. That intrigued me and I texted him. In fact, we texted back and forth a couple of times, but again, that was it.

Later that afternoon we parked the car on a steep hill outside Runyon Canyon. My parents walked at their own pace while I jogged through the park. The air was fresh, my mind was at ease, and when I spotted the Hollywood sign, I thought, *This is going to be my time to shine. This is when all the other acting classes and stage combat training will come together. I am either going to be an actress or do stunt work*. Both those desires were still secrets that only my parents and the other people in the classes knew about. I had promised myself I would only let people know what I had been doing once I got an acting role.

On Wednesday night at an acting school in Burbank, where I had previously taken classes, the instructor was going to give an overview of his upcoming class. I knew I had to see him because he was one of the reasons I never gave up on my acting dreams. He always taught us to dress up, especially if you have an audition. "Dress like you are going on a date," he would tell us.

Usually I got ready in fifteen minutes, but because I wanted to look nice so I would feel good, it took a little longer. Two years prior, I never dressed up for his classes because to get there I had to ride a bike from North Hollywood to Burbank. Riding a bike makes it difficult to wear the shoes and clothes you want.

That night in Burbank, however, I curled my blonde hair, took time deciding on my wardrobe, wore two colours of lipstick—I'm a Pisces and that's what we do—and put on a nice pair of heels I had bought earlier that day.

It made me very happy that night when my mom told me, "You look nice."

Wednesday night the crescent moon was out in Burbank as I trounced up the sidewalk to the acting studio in my heels. My hand excitedly grabbed the handle on the door with clear glass, and when I opened the door, there he was, dressed coolly in soft denim and a casual dress shirt. He was over six feet tall and had soft curly hair. His personality always brought light to the room. He made you feel beautiful, although not so much physically as emotionally. And if people had good character, he picked up on that. He liked people who were genuine, kind, and nice. I once saw him tell a girl to go back to her roots, to be the way she was *before* she came to class, to be the same girl who brought fruit kabobs to share with the students, to be herself and not be all "Hollywood."

According to the Urban Dictionary, Hollywood is "the place where actors and actresses lose their souls, fake emotions, make drama, and earn money for no apparent reason." I think that teacher wanted to make sure his students didn't end up fitting into that definition. Instead he wanted us to remember who we were and use the best parts of ourselves to become great actors.

That night, his eyes sparkled and shone like the moonlight. His laugh was contagious and the smile lines around his eyes were proof of the amount of joy he brought to people. His positive approach always made you want to be better. He'd worked more than thirty years in the industry, including seven years on the set of *Friends*, reading lines whenever the actors playing Joey, Ross, or Chandler were away.

I sat among all the other students in the room, but then his bright eyes caught sight of me. "Glad to see you. Still kicking ass?"

He remembered that I did taekwondo. I nodded as I quietly replied, "Yes. Glad to see you, too."

I was surprised when he seemed to remember me. Although, during our one-on-one session two years before, he told me I reminded him of a renowned actress he had worked with.

At some point during his talk, he again said, "Really good to see you." Then, still looking directly at me, he said, "Sometimes we just need time away." My face was flush, and I smiled as I thought to myself, *Sometimes we do just need time away from the chaos of L.A., but I am back now.*

Even in that room full of people, he still found a way to make me feel good.

I knew that instructor loved beautiful shoes, so after his talk at the studio I told him how I also loved shoes but that I couldn't wear them when I previously took his class. *You can't ride a bike while wearing heels.* Then, when I reminded him how I used to bike from North Hollywood to Burbank for his class on Saturday mornings, he smiled and said, "I look forward to seeing your collection." The words innocently danced out of his mouth.

"Aw, I don't have that many here."

His bright eyes looked at me from six feet in the air, and he smiled as he said, "We're going to work on that."

He wasn't only an acting coach, but also a talent manager in L.A., and I knew he was really going to help me.

And then I never saw his smiling, glowing face again.

Thursday

The next day my parents and I stopped at Patys Restaurant, a 1960s diner with great breakfasts. After breakfast, we went to Trader Joe's to pick up some groceries. Trader Joe's has some of the most unique grocery products I'd ever seen. Having worked in that industry, it was easy for me to spot exclusive products.

That night, with my pen and notepad in the case Dad had duct taped for me, I left the apartment and proceeded to a different acting class. That one was the Meisner course that I needed to complete in order to finish the two-year program. Luckily, the full-time program that I was joining started right where I'd left off in the intensive. I had already achieved Level One, and knew that finishing the program would help me get an acting part. My goal to take acting at two different schools meant attending classes three nights a week.

My Sunfire pulled up outside the theatre in North Hollywood. As my legs carried me across the street, memories began to resurface about how that instructor made you relive your childhood. At that moment I wanted to be the best actress I could, as quickly as I could, just like how I'd become a top gymnast within two years and had won the Top Level One Gymnast Award at the age of nine. I wanted the competitiveness and strength from my childhood to carry onto the stage so I could be at the top of my game.

My mind felt at ease, but as we sat in the dark on the maroon seats waiting for the Meisner class to begin, it happened. All of a sudden a switch went off in my brain, just like those metal chains you pull to turn on a light. "Click" and I was in a different world, a world where other actors and actresses could read my mind and I could read theirs. No one had a clue about what I was thinking and feeling, and all I remember is writing down what the teacher told me about the Meisner technique.

I was up against the truths of my situation—the illness resurfacing and my desire to act. My two biggest secrets had collided head to head in L.A. *What if I had done this? What if I had done that?* But it was too late. My mind was in a psychosis.

Nobody can stop me once my mind "clicks" over into this other world and goes astray. My mind thought everything was going to go right and that everything would work out, but it didn't. After class I drove around for about fifteen minutes because I was so excited about my new world of reading minds. When I finally got back to the apartment, my mind would not let me sleep. Excitement filled my body. Swallowing a sleeping pill did nothing, so I popped another one. It also did nothing. My eyes were fully open and my body and mind were awake most of the night.

Friday

On the morning of Friday January 7, 2011, I drove my parents to the airport. As I was driving, thoughts of various American cities were racing through my mind, almost as fast as that one summer day in grade one when I beat all the boys and girls in my class in an eight-hundred-metre race and clocked over the top hundredth percentile for my age. The thoughts were so distracting that halfway to the airport, I stopped the car on the side of the road, mentioned something about the traffic, and asked my dad to drive. Unfortunately, my parents didn't recognize anything was wrong with me because I was hiding it so well. In retrospect, however, it was a clear sign that something was amiss.

My dad is compassionate toward his family, and the most loyal guy you will ever meet. He is Ukrainian, and a colourful character who tells you how it is. You always know where you stand with him because he always *lets* you know. He sold insurance most of his life and was ahead of his time in the industry. My mom says he is like the character Crankshaft in the comic strip because he twists his words in funny ways or he makes up new words. I call those words "dadisms."

Sometimes he twists words on purpose, and other times he does it just because. He used to call my friend Travis "Trevor," and once when he was talking about wine, instead of saying bouquet, he said "boutique." He would also say "ex-per-ment" instead of experiment, and once after watching a television program about crocodile hunting, he said "Gluck" instead of "Glock."

My childhood was full of colouring, drawing, arts, crafts, athletics, performances, and music. My mom also taught me to be compassionate, loyal, and empathetic. She believed that gossiping about anything can cause quick judgements that are neither valid nor true. Mom stands five feet eight and a half, slightly taller than Dad. She has a mix of Swedish, Scottish, and some other European ancestry, which accounts for her slim build, light blondish short hair, high cheekbones, and light eyes. She also wears wire-framed glasses. My dad taught me mental toughness and to look at details. He taught me to look at landmarks while you are driving so you know where you are going. He also taught me other things like reading the fine print on a form before you sign it and stroking a line through the form if you don't agree with it.

Sadly, on that beautiful, sunny day, my loving, caring, devoted parents left L.A. on their one-way flight home. Thinking back, I needed help but just couldn't tell them what was going on in my head. You see, when I start to become manic I don't know that I am ill; the illness just creeps up on me. I may be reading minds or have American cities flying through my head, but I just think that is normal and a part of me. I can't tell anyone what I am thinking, and I can't decipher when my thoughts are real and when they are manic. In my heart, however, I didn't want my parents to leave, and cried most of the way back to the apartment from the L.A. International Airport.

If I Could Choose

One of my greatest problems is my illness, which can be debilitating to the point of no return. When I am ill my brain has its own story going on. When I am manic, my body has to deal with one thought after another racing through my brain. And because I never share my thoughts with anyone, there is never any release; there is only constant suffering until the situation resolves itself.

My taekwondo instructor used to tell us to adapt and overcome a situation, but my situation is not so easy to adapt to. People don't take the time to understand how much strength it takes for an individual with mental illness to survive. I have to push myself past the side effects from the medication—weight gain, not sleeping well, no energy. I have to motivate myself just to live. I push myself every day to be better. It is not easy at all.

If I could, I would choose to not have this illness. I would choose to not have to hide from it or run from it. I would choose to be free.

CHAPTER 2

A Completely Different Story

This next part of my story is the hardest to explain, and whenever I do, it pulls on my heart strings. When my mind is in a manic state it has a completely different story mapped out. I still see everything and hear everything that is happening, but I might think it means something else. I might feel invincible, or that I can fly like a bird, or there is an underground drug trafficking tunnel right under my feet. Then everything gets combined, reality and non-reality, and in my mind it is all real and it is all happening now.

Re-telling my story here is shameful and makes me feel as though I am living it all over again. While explaining this story to someone who I thought was a friend, he said, "You were really far gone."

Thank you, yes, I know I was, but why can't you see the turmoil this illness puts me through instead of just seeing the insanity?

I hate to tell my story because it hurts so bad, but that is exactly why I have to tell my story.

A Bad Neighbourhood

It was a dark night in Burbank. My black case was on the passenger seat of my car, and as soon as I unlocked the orange Club on my steering wheel, my '97 Sunfire was in motion. My mind told me I was an undercover police officer on a mission to follow people who were suspects. When I'm having a manic episode, my bipolar mind goes astray and I can be anyone I want to be.

I immediately focused on my first target, and my Sunfire accelerated and followed a Thunderbird as the driver stepped on it. My car kept up with him and even followed him into a McDonald's parking lot, but then I decided he wasn't the one I was looking for. My next suspect was a guy who had a Patriots sticker on his car. Bingo! The Patriots sticker was a sign that he would lead me to the right suspects. My brother Michael liked the Patriots, so my mind knew I was headed in the right direction. My Sunfire followed the vehicle into a residential area. My mind identified the suspect as Eric.

My original goal with the black case was to use it as a purse to carry items to my acting classes, as well as a prop on stage if I needed one. But that night the case helped with my undercover get-up. When I arrived at the foot of the driveway of the strange house where the car with the Patriots sticker was parked, I saw Eric look back before walking into the garage. My hand picked up my black case and my feet stepped out of the Sunfire. As I followed him into the garage, I made a mental note that he was about six foot one with a medium build and shaved dirty blonde hair.

Inside the garage was a barber shop. That was not in my head; it was actually there. Eric was sitting on a three-seater 1960s floral couch set at a diagonal in the garage. Henry stood five foot three and had slicked-back dark hair. He was cutting the hair of another guy sitting in a red barbershop chair. When I looked slightly to the right, my eyes caught site of a four-by-two picture hanging on the wall. There hung a $1,000 bill that bore the face of Miguel Lopez.

As I walked further into the garage, a.k.a. the barbershop, I held my case in the air and called out, "I've got a Gluck and I'm not afraid to use it."

Henry's eyes widened. "Where did she come from?"

Eric calmly replied, "I don't know. She just followed me up the driveway."

I then sat with my right foot on top of my left quadriceps on the couch at the opposite end to Eric. I asked Henry, "What are you going to do?"

Henry was pacing back and forth and seemed a little freaked out. Suddenly, he pulled out a black portable phone and motioned it at me. "Why don't you call the cops?"

I glared at him. "Why would *I* call the cops? Why don't *you* call the cops?"

And he did.

It was perfect. Henry, who my mind thought was a drug dealer, had just called the cops to his house. He had busted himself. From the couch, Eric pointed to the $1,000 bill picture on the wall. My eyes looked in that direction.

"That's funky," I commented, as crickets chirped in the background.

Eric responded, "Exactly what I thought."

When Karl, an African American guy in his twenties, came out of the house and walked into the garage, I pushed myself up from the couch, white knuckled my black case, and stuck it in the air.

"I've got a Gluck and I'm going to blow this bitch down."

Karl's face went pale, his expression deadpan, and his hands went straight up in the air. "Where did this girl come from?" he cried out. When he saw that no one else had their hands up, he dropped them and said, "I'm out of here." He took off, walking quickly down the driveway.

Then the face from the picture on the wall entered the garage from the house. He stood at least six feet tall with greased hair.

"I'm Miguel Lopez and I own this house," he explained. "You have to leave."

When my foot kicked a pile of cement bags in the corner, one of them opened and sent cement dust flying in the air. My legs proceeded to walk down the driveway with my case in hand. I got into the Sunfire and drove across the street and up the neighbour's driveway. I parked and got out of the car.

In my manic mind the whole block was a drug dealing street. I threw my orange Club into the neighbour's yard. It bounced on the lawn. My mind thought it was marking where the drugs were hidden underground so that when the cops came, they would know where to look. Then I went behind the garage, and one of my arms picked up a lead pipe while the other picked up a brick. My arm hurled the brick away and almost smashed the back windshield of an SUV at the end of another driveway. Then my finger punched a code into what I thought was a mailbox beside me; I believed the code was going to do something to the underground drug area. Shortly after that, I got into the car, my foot stepped on the gas pedal, and my Sunfire left the neighbourhood.

As I drove my car out of the area that my mind thought was a drug trafficking street, I was pulled over by the police. There was a lineup of cars on the side of the road, and when a police officer approached the Sunfire, I rolled down the window. He told me to get out of the vehicle, but instead I tried to run. I can't tell you why I tried to run at the time, considering my mind thought I was an undercover police officer. In any case, he grabbed me and cuffed me without any explanation at all.

Then a different officer in his forties began yelling and spraying spit in my face as he went off on a rant. "Why are you trying to run away from the police? You have to obey the law. What are you doing running away?"

My shoulders shrugged.

He then asked, "Where are you living?"

My voice squeaked the name of the street where I was staying.

The officer spouted with more spit. "You are a long way from there. You cannot run away from a police officer. It is my duty to keep the streets clean. Do you understand me?"

My head nodded yes.

He continued to lecture me for a while, and then asked, "Can I give you a breathalyzer?"

I answered, "Yes."

When he checked the breathalyzer, he simply said, "Woo, woo. She blew a double zero." The police then took off the handcuffs and let me go.

After I parked my Sunfire back behind the building where I was staying, I casually headed up to my apartment. I left my door wide open as I started singing songs with profanities in them. I was listening to a song by R & B singer Eamon with the headphone from my MP3 player in one ear as I yelled the lyrics of the first two lines out the open door. Two f-bombs, some song lyrics, and an s-sharp ricocheted in the courtyard.

I looked down to see the lady who owned the building standing on the ground floor. Her stern voice, straight dark blonde hair, and dark eyes were all telling me, "Please be respectful of the other people living here."

I ignored her.

My mind thought the words to the song had some hidden meaning and that my voice was trying to relay a message to someone there. My voice echoed in the courtyard with the next two lines of the R & B song which included two more f-bombs and lyrics about a hoe.

Again, I heard, "Excuse me, you have to be respectful of the building and the other people living here."

My mouth spit out two more lines containing profanities and the words boomeranged around the courtyard.

And again, a little louder and more insistent, "You have to respect the other people here."

Eventually I apologized and my hand shut the door. While I'm manic I'm not often nasty, but I can be irritable, uncooperative, and guarded. I also don't usually yell or swear unless I'm manic, but that would explain why I was singing songs with swear words. Clearly, my mind wasn't operating well, and after everything that happened at the house and with the police, I needed some form of release.

Inside the apartment I had this sense that somebody had been inside. My mind did not feel at ease. My brain sensed that people had used the shower and slept on the twin bed while I was away. I cleaned the shower with whatever was handy, then removed the sheets from the twin bed, and opened the door and placed them outside. I could not sleep with those sheets in the same room. Finally, I shut the door, and my mind and body went to sleep.

Saturday

The next morning I went down to the laundry room to clean and purge the evil sheets of germs from the people who had been prowling around in my apartment while I was out the night before. There was a guy there, and I talked to him as I rummaged through my purse to find change for the washer.

Back upstairs, I grabbed my backpack filled with items I needed for my Meisner class and went for a drive.

Peeling into a neighbourhood, my Sunfire pulled into another stranger's driveway. My arm threw my car in park and picked up the lead pipe still sitting on the front seat. I climbed out of the car and with the arm-shaped pipe started tearing down the stranger's nicely pruned bushes that grew against his fence. My mind told me this was a huge drug house that was concocting drugs in the basement. My mind also told me that drugs were being made underground in an assembly line throughout the neighbourhood.

A Caucasian stranger came out of the house. He was in his sixties, had patches of grey hair, and wore a hat and a red shirt emblazoned with the NBC logo. When he looked at me, he narrowed his eyes, and said, "What are you doing here? This is private property."

My mind told me the stranger was my dad's stepdad who never used to listen or hear people. My voice got loud. "You need to open your ears."

The stranger clenched his fists and his face turned red. "You shouldn't be here right now."

Another person came out of the house next door.

When I'm in a manic state I am not afraid of anything, so instead of leaving, I climbed onto the ledge of my Sunfire so

I could be eye to eye with the man. My voice got even louder. "Don't you understand? People have been trying to tell you for years that you need to listen and you never do. Maybe if you opened your ears you would understand."

Then the man slapped me hard across the face.

Stunned, I grabbed my face and exclaimed, "Oh my God, you just hit me."

Then I turned toward the neighbour, who had walked into the man's yard and was standing just a few feet away from me. "He just hit me!" I yelled.

My cheek hurt and had begun to swell. I struggled to close the door of my Sunfire, but the man wouldn't let me.

The neighbour nervously interjected. "Why don't you walk with me? We can talk. I like music. Do you like music?"

My voice went up a pitch. "I can *play* music. I have a recorder."

The recorder was in my backpack in the trunk of the Sunfire. I kept it for my Meisner acting class in case we had to do activities during our scenes. I opened the back of the car, pulled out the backpack, placed it on the road, and removed the recorder. I started playing the Christmas song "What Child is This?" It was a song I played in music class when I was a child, and the song I could play the best.

The neighbour hummed along, and when I was finished playing, he said, "Music is good."

By then, other neighbours were also outside watching. They didn't approach me or say anything to me, probably because they were shocked and stunned by everything that was going on and neither willing nor able to do anything.

I placed the recorder back in the backpack and the backpack into my trunk. Then I walked over to the road between the stranger's house and another neighbour's house, knelt down, and lay flat on the road. With my hands stretched out above my head, my body started barrel rolling across the ground. In my mind there was an underground tunnel to where the stranger and his neighbours had a drug operation going on. I started yelling "Michael knows, Michael knows" because in my mind my brother knew how to access the neighbourhood drug operation.

The police showing up is exactly what my mind hoped for. My body barrel rolling was revealing the exact location that would lead to the police busting the neighbourhood drug operation, or so my mind thought. But when the police arrived, they didn't seem interested in why I was doing what I was doing, and I didn't get a chance to tell them.

Any other individual observing the situation of me barrel rolling and yelling some guy's name would have thought I was in desperate need for help. Maybe the officer who arrested me wasn't trained properly, or maybe he had it in for people like me. Either way, he did not do what he should have done, and that led to a lot of unnecessary pain and trauma for me and my family.

CHAPTER 3

5150 of the California Welfare and Institutions Code

If an individual is participating in strange activities such as barrel rolling across the ground, they should be taken in on a 5150. Also known as an involuntary psychiatric hold, a 5150 is a section of the California Welfare and Institutions Code (Thomson Reuters, 2017). It authorizes a mental health practitioner or an officer to involuntarily confine an individual suspected to have a mental disorder who are either gravely disabled, a danger to themselves, or a danger to others. The individual can be brought into custody for up to seventy-two hours for assessment or placed into a treatment facility.

The best thing anyone could have done for me that day was take me to see a mental health practitioner, but judging by the fact that those officers in L.A. chose to arrest me instead of getting me the mental health care I needed, especially after witnessing my bizarre behaviour, seems to indicate I wasn't the first person that had happened to.

Instead of giving me a 5150 and one of the officers saying, "You are not under arrest, but I am taking you for an examination by a mental health professional," they cuffed me, shackled me, and put me in the back of a police car without telling me my rights.

The instant I was put in the car, "Poof." My mind thought of someone I knew who had been arrested when they were mentally ill and had kicked the window out of a police car. I thought the incident should be repeated. So while lying down in the back seat of the cruiser, my feet popped the window right out of the frame. It didn't even break.

When the police officer asked, "Why did you kick the window out of the car?" My mind couldn't tell him the real reason. Instead, my head jolted up from lying down and blurted out, "Because I have to take a piss-piss."

Piss-piss, you ask? That is a dadism that I wouldn't normally say, but when I am manic, I can lose my filter.

The police officer in the passenger seat replied, "That sounds like the name of a bar."

I was about to respond when my eyes widened in surprise. My Sunfire was being towed up onto a large tow truck with a massive ramp and the name Archer's Tow stamped on the side. As the police car began to drive away, my mouth opened and out came the words, "Can I please go to my acting class?"

The officer asked, "Where is your acting class?"

I gave him the exact name and address of the acting school, but instead of going to my Meisner class I ended up at the North Hollywood Police Station. There was a wait for the restroom, and I really needed to go pee because my bladder was hurting. I wasn't scared because when I'm manic I often feel invincible. However, I could hear jail cell doors clanking, and I felt cold.

After finishing in the restroom the police officer motioned me into a tiny jail cell. A female officer then told me to keep my hands behind my back. When she recuffed me, my voice shook in pain.

"Ouch! You're hurting me. Why are you hurting me?" Even though I wasn't resisting, she was still being aggressive.

Then she turned me around and reached down to start ripping my shoelaces from my new suede calf-high off-white Steve Madden boots. I asked her what she was doing.

"It is standard procedure to remove your shoelaces."

Less than an hour later, they brought me before an officer I hadn't talked to at the North Hollywood Police Station. Taller than me, stocky, and with short blonde hair, he didn't say a single word to me. He simply looked me up and down, and uttered, "Book her."

The reason they booked me in jail was due to the vandalism of the police car window. As for the original arrest, it would have been because I was "disturbing the peace" in the neighbourhood. Someone must have called them. Probably one of the drug dealers.

Not for Everyone

In 2016, Kanye West was picked up in the state of California on a 5150. I was at my aunt and uncle's house in Calgary, Canada when the 5150 news came on the television. My Uncle Doug who is usually comical and even-tempered immediately angrily stated "Why does he get a 5150 and you didn't?"

Hearing that instantly made my heart ache and terrible flashbacks of me going to jail resurfaced. Then I searched for other celebrities who were able to get a 5150: Britney Spears,

Amanda Bynes, Mischa Barton to name a few. They were all celebrities; I was not. My life might have taken a different direction and certainly would have entailed less pain if the police had taken me to see a mental health professional when they saw me barrel rolling across the ground.

That the celebrities didn't go to jail raises a number of questions. Why was the 5150 law created if not to secure help for the mentally ill? Was it specifically to give celebrities an easier way of navigating the system? Why is the system so off balance? Why are more individuals not taken in on a 5150? Are mentally ill individuals pushed through the system to make money? Why did I not get the help that I so deserved?

In my case, the police officer who arrested me knew I was either a mental health patient, under the care of a mental health professional, or that my behaviour suggested a mental disorder. And I know that because he marked it on the Arrestee Medical Screening Form.

Cell Transfer

From North Hollywood Police Station they drove me in a police car to Van Nuys Station. They took me from the car cuffed and shackled into a room with a huge glass window to get my mugshot. It seemed more like a jail than a station. I wasn't scared, even though there were two older criminal women on either side of me—one in her forties with red curly hair and one in her fifties. They both wore orange jumpsuits, and the three of us sat on a bench. Waiting in a glass room beside us were four criminal men—a blond Caucasian in his twenties, an African American in his fifties, another African American in his thirties, and a young Caucasian with short dark hair. Normally you would think since I come from a good family, had never been to jail, and hadn't done drugs or gotten drunk that I would be terrified in that situation, but because my mind wasn't functioning properly, nothing bothered me. Eventually the camera flashed and I rolled my eyes to the back of my head. My mugshot was done.

Near the fingerprinting station was an open area. While I waited there, one of the police officers went through my wallet and found my psychiatrist's business card from Winnipeg. He asked, "What's this for?"

My answer was, "Talk therapy."

The officer seemed more concerned with counting my money, of which I only had about $50. He sighed, "I keep getting it wrong." He had to count my money at least three times. Instead of doing that, he should have been getting me medical attention. He should have called my psychiatrist.

After an Asian officer in his thirties took my fingerprints, they put me into a cell with a small area elevated about a foot off the ground. The whole floor was painted grey and it was dingy. In the corner was a dark blue body bag, or so my mind thought. In fact it was an LAPD oversized pillow case, but I thought it was a body bag because I could tell my entire body would fit into it. That made me think it was used to transport criminals in and out of jail.

Locked inside the dark, dingy, grey cell, I didn't know why I was there or what was going on. My mind helped me escape the jail system by practising dialogue from an acting class scene. In my Meisner class we were taught to go to our animal instincts. The instructor, Barry, always talked about martial arts and the praying mantis. That made me reminisce about competing in taekwondo and the confidence I had back then. My mind thought about Barry when I was in jail because while on stage during his class he made me feel powerful, positive, and eager to fight for the strength I had inside me. Those feelings and my inner strength helped get me through the days spent in lockdown.

Hissing Like a Snake

I felt tension in the air and decided to tap into my animal instincts. My arms whipped the dark blue body bag back and forth, only stopping when people walked by so I could hiss like a snake. Why a snake? Because I am terrified of them and thought they would scare the people away.

Acting was in the forefront of my brain while I was in jail. I remembered everything I was taught and I was in character the whole time. I used my animal instincts to show people how I felt on the inside and to scare them away. My arms continued to whip the body bag in the air, back and forth, side to side, as high as it could go. I took what Barry taught me and found safety in it. I used it to protect myself from the harmful jail system.

The Doctor

A few hours later, an officer escorted me to see a doctor on staff. He asked me, "Why do you see a psychiatrist?"

Again my answer was, "Talk therapy."

At the time I wasn't on any medication. That doctor did nothing for me besides ask a couple of questions and send me back to my cell. What he should have done was provide proper medical attention, or, at the very least, called my psychiatrist. They found his telephone number and contact information on his business card in my wallet, but they did nothing with it.

Looking back, what I needed was somebody to explain about my illness. Somebody to care and take the time to tell me I was mentally ill and the only way I would get better was if I took medication. When I am manic I do not comprehend that I am mentally ill. So I needed someone to tell me that I could choose to take the medication and become well or continue without treatment and suffer the consequences of the illness. Why didn't somebody simply understand that I needed help in a big way and needed care and support? Instead I was sent packing back to my cell with no choices and no explanations.

How that system was run with a doctor like that made it seem obvious that they were praying on the ill and only wanted to make money off them. Otherwise there would be a better plan in place for the mentally ill.

Try to imagine your brain is not operating correctly and you're thinking of multiple other thoughts. Now imagine the pressure of the lock-down, the slamming of the bars, the cold, grey concrete, the handcuffs, the shackles, the prints, the mugshot, and the guards' thick clunky boots adding pressure to your confined, unwell mental status. The prison system in the United States is so wretched and heart-shattering because it's a revolving door for many suffering with mental illness. This in turn creates a stress, a trouble, a pain, a torment on top of your already traumatic illness.

Can nobody else see the unwelcome and detrimental effects?

The Phone Call

Several hours later, one of the guards wheeled up a payphone close to my cell. It took hours before my hand reached out for the phone through those metal bars because I was busy whipping the body bag around. Then it occurred to me that I needed to let my parents know where I was.

According to the California Code, Penal Code–PEN 851.5 Section (a)(1), "Immediately upon being booked and, except where physically impossible, no later than three hours after arrest, an arrested person has the right to make at least three completed telephone calls . . ." (Thomson Reuters, 2017).

And that means someone in that jail system should have brought me the phone long before they did.

In a later session back in Winnipeg with my psychiatrist I vocalized how lucky I was to be able to make that phone call with my mind being astray, but he didn't think it was all about luck. I can't quote his exact words because some of our sessions were so powerful I can only process them in the moment. Even by the time my mind had processed his words it was hard to remember exactly what he said because I was working against a difficult situation, and as I talked it through, my eyes were full of tears. Even as I write this, I have to pause for a brief moment because the tears won't stop and my chest has a stabbing pain. In any case, the way I understood that session with my doctor was that the universe brought my dad and me together on that day, and I believe that to be true.

I am blessed to have my parents who are so supportive of me and will do anything to help me. That is why I often think about that day in Van Nuys Station and wonder what would have happened if my hand hadn't reached through the bars for the phone. Likely, I would have been shuffled around and lost in the system longer than I already was. And that is why I believe I am fortunate to have made that call, that even though my mind was in a psychosis, it still knew to reach out to my parents for help.

Around 12:00 a.m. I was wide awake and couldn't sleep. My hand reached out for the phone to call my dad. It was 2:00 a.m. in Winnipeg. Can you imagine being on the receiving end of that call? I was a decent daughter, a good person, a hard worker who had graduated university. My parents and I had a healthy, loving, supportive relationship. And even though my mind struggled with mental issues for most of my life, I was not a criminal.

My dad was half asleep when he picked up the phone. I heard him say, "Hello?"

The operator said, "You have a collect call from Sandra. Do you accept the charges?"

Without hesitation, he answered, "Yes."

When I was finally on the line, I simply said, "Hi Dad, I'm in jail."

"Where are you?" he asked.

I looked at the paper on the wall of the cell. "I'm in Van Nuys."

"Are you okay?" I could tell he was concerned, yet calm.

"Yes" was all I could say.

He grabbed a pen to write down the details, and before ending the call, he reassured me. "We'll be there tomorrow."

CHAPTER 4

My Happy Childhood

Performance has been part of my existence ever since I was a small child. I loved to make up gymnastics or dance routines outside in our backyard, either by myself or with my friend Karen as my pink cassette deck blasted songs from the movie *Dirty Dancing* or by Paula Abdul. Inside the house I played the piano and sang, sometimes recording myself singing theme songs from my favourite television shows while the TV ran in the background.

If I wasn't singing, dancing, or doing gymnastics, I was playing sports with my brother Michael. In fact, I idolized him and followed him around, doing whatever he did. If he and his friends played football I would join in, tackle them, and drag them across the lawn by their feet. I was a true tomboy. When he skated, I skated. When he learned piano and trumpet, so did I. And because he never drank alcohol, neither did I.

Four years older than me, Michael stands a little more than five foot eleven and has dark wavy hair, sparkling blue eyes, and a lean build. His killer smile is the result of braces during his teenage years. He always helps people, and I love his genuine, compassionate, caring, and good-hearted nature—he got that from our parents. His intelligence mesmerizes me still. The way he can explain things three different ways so that I can understand is mind boggling. I always wanted to be "just like Mike."

As a child, I was generally quiet, soft-spoken, and easy going. And I spent so much time outside in the sunlight playing sports or dancing that my hair was bleached blonde, the perfect complement to my tanned skin and green eyes.

When I was young, my mom jokingly called me "the bag lady" because I liked to dress up in layers of clothing and I always carried around extra outfits in whatever type of bag I could get my hands on. Plastic, cloth, vinyl—you name it. My wardrobe was always packed with lots of different clothes, and Mom would say that I dressed myself as soon as I came out of the womb. If there was a basket of laundry somewhere, I would dive into it and wrap the clothing around me, making many wardrobe changes. Often when we went to the mall, I wore hand-me-down dresses that were too long. If we saw people she knew, I could tell Mom was a bit embarrassed by my attire, but she never told me "don't wear that." She let me do my thing.

When I was five years old we moved into a new split-level house in a neighbourhood outside of Winnipeg. There was an old antique buffet on the main level that my dad refinished and a black shiny piano in the entrance. Mom often cooked dinner after work and the sweet aroma hung in the air throughout the home. My dad fixed everything and anything, and often helped out the neighbours if they needed their lawn cut or snow shovelled. Dad had a keen eye for observing everything, and bluntly told people what he thought; Mom was more reserved, compassionate, and kept things to herself. She knew how to read music and play the piano; music was always a part of our lives.

Our parents were consistently there for Michael and me. They supported us, loved us, and took care of us. They worked hard at their occupations—Mom as a nurse and Dad in sales—and always completed any task they started. After work they would drive us to our extra-curricular activities and watch our sporting games and competitions. Dad used to help Michael play hockey from the stands by shooting with him or body-checking for him. Our parents taught us to be competitive and do everything to our best ability. They encouraged us to be the best we could in every task we took on.

Michael and I hardly ever fought with each other, unless he teased me. He used to sing, "Sandra, stoungy, stew takes a poo, pees her pants, adores her aunts and eats them, too." That made me so mad I often squealed at him. My parents never allowed us to use the word *bored*, insisting instead that we find something to do, like go outside and play, practise a musical instrument, or do a craft.

Sometimes my parents struggled to pay for my gymnastics and my brother's tier hockey, but they never said anything. Even when there was hardly enough money to scrape together, they still carried us through and never let us know times were tough. They always helped us in any way they possibly could. As a family we got along extremely well and always looked out for each other.

At the age of seven a new elementary school was built right across the street from our house. I could cartwheel to school in thirty seconds. In grade three I started gymnastics, training three times a week. I wore a hand-me-down competition body suit that was blue with a yellow and white stripe that made a V-shape in the front. Karen started in gymnastics when she was a bit younger than me, so she taught me how to do my first back handspring. In grade four I won an all-around gymnastics competition in Portage la Prairie, an hour away from my house. The gym smelt of chalk dust and I was both nervous and excited to compete. It was the first all-around I won that year. To most people it's only a piece of gold dangling from your neck, but to me it's a happy childhood moment that continued to trigger over and over again.

The next competition was Provincials. Because of my last win, I wore an air of cocky confidence as I walked past all the gymnasts from the other schools. Unfortunately, I was one of the last to go on all the events, which made me very nervous. My gymnastics instructor tried to move me up in the rotation order, but I was not allowed. That affected my performance, and I only placed third in that competition.

In 1988, at the end of the gymnastics year, I was the top Level 1 gymnast at my club; I was very proud of my achievements. However, when the club moved me up to the National level the next year, that meant five days a week of gymnastics in grade five. All I did was go to school, do homework, and do gymnastics. I had no social life and soon dropped out. During elementary school I beat all the boys in my classes at long distance running races, and in grade six I played soccer with the boys at recess. I was still a tomboy.

Because I had good marks and excelled in the regular school programs, I was placed in a gifted program with other students from my school. We were taken outside our regular classroom to study phobias. Each day we learned about a different one, but I didn't understand why we were learning about phobias at all, let alone why we had to miss our regular course work to do so. I often asked myself, *Why not grade seven math or something to get ahead?* Eventually, I spoke up about my concerns, and shortly afterward, the gifted program stopped. I'm not sure if that had anything to do with me, but I always stood up for what I believed was right, and I know that stopping that program was the right thing to do.

In grades seven and eight I no longer cartwheeled to school. I was in junior high, and because that school was further away from home, I had to take a bus. By then, my teeth had braces with black elastics, my hair was brunette and reached down to the middle of my back, and acne had flared up and covered most of my face. I played trumpet, piano, and any sport I could. Because the trumpet hurt to play with braces, I used special dental wax on my teeth. In basketball I played point-guard and aggressively peeled the ball out of opponents' hands, sometimes swinging girls around by the ball. I won free-throwing competitions, the basketball award, and an academic award. One would think from all these achievements that my self-esteem would have been at an all-time high, but I actually wanted to crawl into a hole and hide. In grade eight I was on every acne medication and pill possible to clear up my complexion, but nothing worked.

The summer after grade eight I volunteered fulltime from Monday to Friday at the hospital where my mom worked as a nurse. My acne was still really bad and I tried to cover it up with make-up, but that didn't work either. Although my self-esteem suffered because of my looks, I pushed myself to go out and do things. I didn't hide. I volunteered in a gift shop and served beverages at a stand-up coffee shop to the doctors and nurses who passed through the line. A paid worker in the coffee shop was nasty and rude to me, always undermining me and being unpleasant in the way she told me to do tasks. I tried to ignore her, but she made me feel shallow and low. My parents listened to what I said about her every day and they sincerely empathized with me. That's when they taught me to write things down and record what people said when they didn't treat me fairly.

By grade nine I had tried every possible acne cream, gel, and medication, except one. Then, in 1993, my dermatologist prescribed me the acne isotretinoin drug Accutane. It was my last hope at beautiful skin. Within a couple of months the acne had cleared up, and I no longer had to try and cover it up with make-up. My skin was finally beautiful.

The Snake

Soon after I started to feel better about my appearance, one of my teachers began sharing inappropriate sexual content during his Language Arts course. It really upset me and made me feel bad.

One afternoon he was talking about a poem when he said, "A snake going up a drain pipe." Then he asked the class, "Do you know what this represents?" When nobody said anything, the teacher responded, "This represents this guy not getting his sexual fulfillment as a child because he was mommy's little boy." I didn't understand why he had said that or even why he was sharing that particular poem with us. And it wasn't the last time he included sexual content in his course; in fact, he did it as often as he could.

I can't say for sure, but I think this might have launched my fear of snakes, all because of a grubby little teacher and his disgusting thoughts.

I knew that what he was doing was wrong, so I wrote down all of his inappropriate comments with the exact time and date he said them. Because of how I was mistreated by the worker while I volunteered in the summer, I knew exactly what to do this time. I complained to the principal and the guidance counsellor about his behaviour. The principal sat in on our class two or three times, but, of course, the teacher did nothing while the principal was there. Then the principal tried to re-arrange my schedule so I didn't have any classes with that teacher, but once again, it affected my regular school schedule. I didn't understand why *my* learning should suffer because of *his* behaviour, and I decided to stick out the year with that teacher. When my parents and I reported him to Child and Family Services, the head doctor there said what the teacher was doing was "manifestly uncool," but that's as far as it went. Nothing happened to that pervert teacher during my last year of junior high, but the next year he didn't teach at that school.

That was not the first time I challenged a system, and it would not be the last.

Time for a Change

I thrived on change and variety, and by the end of grade nine after everything that had happened with that teacher, I made the decision to go to a different high school and leave everyone in junior high behind. I transferred to Miles Macdonell Collegiate where I undertook the International Baccalaureate program in advanced science and math. I played piano and trumpet, studied Royal Conservatory written music, and was involved in every sport I could.

I met a new friend while playing basketball. Keira was a year older than me, and had curly long blonde hair and blue eyes. In the beginning, I could tell she didn't like me, but I didn't know why. Our interactions were so limited there didn't seem to be anything she could possibly dislike about me. Eventually, however, she started talking to me on a regular basis, and that's when I learned the reason for her chilly demeanour. She had thought I liked Jason, the same guy she liked. If she'd asked me right at the beginning, I would have told her that I was still a bit of a tomboy and even though I had a lot of guy friends, I had no romantic feelings whatsoever for any of them, including Jason. Keira also told me that I flirted with girls the same way I flirted with guys. She said, "You talk to everyone the same." That's when she knew for sure I did not like Jason.

I also met the twins Larissa and Melanie in high school and we hung around all the time. They were not identical—Melanie was shorter than her sister—but they were both pretty and had long hair. Melanie and I were point guards on the basketball team. The three of us would go together to house parties and parks, and despite being underage, Larissa and I even tried to sneak into bars. Sometimes we got in and sometimes we were turned away.

I was fifteen when I got my beginner's licence and started taking driver's ed. I liked the idea of being independent and not having to rely on my parents or friends or public transport to take me where I wanted to go. And driving seemed like fun, so it was really disappointing when I failed my first driver's test. They told me if I took more training, I could test again in two months. I was determined not to fail again. I finally got my licence when I was sixteen, and it felt great.

In addition to school and sports and friends, I also earned some money by working part-time jobs. Initially I was a server at Taco Bell, and then a building attendant for the River East School Division, of which Miles Macdonell was a part. I had to unlock the schools when groups wanted to use the gym, and then lock up and turn on the alarm when they were finished. I used the time between unlocking and locking up to get my homework done, or to do whatever else I liked.

Life was definitely busy, but it was also fun, and I was happy and enjoying everything life had to offer.

CHAPTER 5

The Start of My Downfall

My friend Andrew used to call me every Sunday. I am very empathetic toward others and can instantly pick up on their energy when I talk to them—something I definitely got from my parents. Andrew and I met a year or so before at a mall; he was from Trinidad and had dark hair, dark eyes, and long eyelashes. He called me because he wanted to talk about things going on in his life and needed someone to listen. When he began calling me three times a week, I was a bit surprised, but still happy to be there for my friend.

One day in early June when Andrew called, I knew right away that something was wrong. We talked for a while until he admitted he had just taken a bunch of pills. He had attempted suicide and only told me. He asked me not to tell anyone, but as soon as I could, I got off the phone and called his childhood friend Shane, who I also knew. Shane immediately called the police and then called me back to let me know the police were on their way to Andrew's house. I found out later that the police had to chase Andrew down a back alley and make him go to the hospital to have his stomach pumped. He told me later that he didn't realize how much everyone cared for him until he tried to kill himself.

Gosh, I could have told you that, Andrew! I believe that if I hadn't called Shane, Andrew could have died.

Andrew's attempted suicide really affected me, and for a long time afterward I talked to anyone I could about it, including my guidance counsellor, people I worked with, and friends and family. That incident was very traumatic and caused me a lot of extra stress in my life, stress that was too difficult for someone of my age to handle. And that was the beginning of my downfall.

The Snake Returns

At the end of grade eleven I ran for Student Council. Keira and I designed a poster and badges. She was my campaign manager, and prior to the speech on Election Day, she and I did a big performance with fourteen other people. I performed gymnastics and break dancing and choreographed the other students' routines. They wore black and had letters pinned to their backsides that spelled out VOTE FOR SANDRA. I received a lot of votes from the grade twelve students because we played sports together. And I was very happy to be elected secretary of the Student Council for my grade twelve year.

Around that time something else happened to stress me out. That snaky teacher I had in junior high came back into the picture. It turned out his adopted son Ethan went to the same high school as me. Ethan was a year older and we used to talk and say hi in the halls. I didn't know who his father was until one day the snaky teacher came by the school and I saw him with Ethan. When that teacher saw me in the halls, I was disgusted and happily ignored him.

But the next time I saw Ethan, he turned cold on me. He wouldn't talk to me and he wouldn't say hi. I realized that snaky teacher must have spoken badly about me to his son. To top it off, Keira told me Ethan's dad was telling people I was an attention seeker. That really ticked me off. The only way he could rationalize his inappropriate sexual behaviours was to call me names. I wasn't seeking attention, though. I simply tried to do the right thing and help other students who couldn't or wouldn't speak up about his foolish remarks. I had to tell Keira my side of the story, not because I wanted to—I was so done with that teacher—but I felt I had to explain to her what a letch he was. Fortunately, she listened and was equally appalled, but it was another stress-provoking situation I didn't need in my life.

Whiplash

One afternoon in June 1996, right after the election, I was driving home from high school in Mom's turquoise two-door Sunbird. Both she and Michael said the colour was actually teal—they had the same sense of humour and thought they were being very funny. Anyway, I was stopped for a pedestrian at a cross-walk on Henderson Highway when a BMW rear-ended me. The impact wrenched my neck and back, and although I didn't need to go to the hospital, I did go to see a chiropractor whose office was only a minute away from where the accident occurred.

When I told him what had happened, he took a look at me before concluding, "You have whiplash." Then he prescribed a treatment plan to help get me back on track.

That incident added to the stress I already had, and the constant pain I endured for quite a while afterward made me suffer a great deal. It all added up to more fuel on the fire of my downfall.

Out of Character

After being elected into student council and after the car accident, I was stressed because of everything that happened and so excited I couldn't sleep. At 3:00 one morning in late June, I was wide awake and flooded with excitement. I kept thinking about how we were only going to be allowed out of class for a couple of hours during Fun Day, and my thoughts were racing. *Why can't it be* all *day?* That's when I had my brilliant idea to get the students an *extended* day full of all sorts of activities.

By 5:00 a.m. I was on the computer downstairs typing a letter about my brilliant idea. And then when I got to school, I used the photocopy machine—one of the perks of being elected to student council—to copy my letter. After I signed it, I also got two others on student council to sign it so my name wouldn't be the only one. Finally, I put copies of the letter in all the staff mailboxes.

After reading the letter, one of the teachers came up to me and said, "You can't do that."

Of course I didn't say anything, but I thought to myself, *I can do anything. I recently saved someone from dying.*

Writing that letter to the staff of my high school gave me so much excitement and energy that it was the start of me doing things I didn't normally do. One day when Melanie and Larissa had a spare period, I decided to skip a class with them. I *never* skipped class. We went to Kildonan Park where people go to showboat their cars. There was a sprinkler going so I ran through it and got all my clothes soaking wet. Melanie and Larissa laughed at my entertainment value. We went to their house so I could change into some dry clothes because my house was too far away. Then we went to my Spanish friend's house, but he wasn't home. Instead, an attractive guy who I didn't know answered the door. Later, with all my energy, excitement, and confidence, I had the brilliant idea to return to my Spanish friend's house. I took a flower with me, and when the attractive guy opened the door, I asked him out. I also got his phone number.

Everything I did that day was completely out of character for me.

Shopping Spree

That weekend I went to the mall. I felt so good about the weight I had lost recently that I went into Le Chateau and tried on a whole lot of clothes that fit my figure and looked good. Feeling satisfied, I went up to the cashier to purchase the clothes. I handed the clerk the credit card my dad gave me to use for gas for the car, but she wouldn't accept it because it wasn't mine. A lady I knew whose daughter was in junior high with me was in the store at the time, and offered to pay for me.

"How much is it?" she asked.

"$400," I replied.

She looked at me and responded, "I can't give you that much."

I was disappointed and left the store without any of the items I had wanted. As I wandered through the mall, I kept thinking about another idea I had of doing a tour of skits on self-esteem and safe sex. A group I was in for Language Arts class had just done a video on peer pressure and I thought that idea could be expanded. All of those thoughts were flying through my brain, and with all my energy driving me, I went into the drug store and bought condoms to give out to people. Then I lay down on the bench in the mall and shut my eyes. A security guard woke me up and told me the mall was closing and I had to leave. When he walked me to my car, I gave him a condom, and said, "This is for safe sex." I wasn't having sex, but my thoughts were if other people were, they should at least be safe.

As I drove away from the mall, I thought people were following me and turned down a back alley to lose them. When I suspected someone else was following me, I stepped on the gas to get rid of them.

When I arrived home, I saw the light flashing on the answering machine. No one else was there, so I listened to the message. It was my brother's friend, and I thought he said he had stopped over, but when I listened to the message again, I realized he hadn't. Then I saw that the green chair down the flight of stairs was turned and facing the opposite direction it usually did, so I thought the friend *had* been at the house earlier. My mind was playing all sorts of tricks on me.

Query Reaction to Accutane

My mind was off kilter and my words were not always making sense. There were a bunch of National Geographic maps in the closet downstairs and I took them all up to my bedroom and placed them all over my walls. One school lunch hour I got pamphlets from a government agency about teen issues, and when I got home I placed them by the telephone in my room. I thought I was going to save the world, just like I had saved Andrew's life. Not only were my thoughts about saving the world, but also about my friends and me touring the world. But I didn't go on tour. Instead, my parents, who had noticed I was saying and doing things that were unusual for me, took me to the Health Sciences Centre in Winnipeg to see a doctor.

The doctor had short salt and pepper hair; he dressed highly sophisticated in my eyes. He began by asking me routine questions. Through the process of elimination, he determined I wasn't suicidal, wasn't drunk or on drugs, wasn't promiscuous, wasn't depressed, and didn't have an eating disorder. And that's when he wrote in the chart, "Query reaction to Accutane."

Accutane

Accutane was the isotretinoin drug I was taking for acne. It was put on the market in 1982 after being approved by the FDA for use in treating severe acne that was unresponsive to conventional therapies. At that time, it was also given a Category X pregnancy rating—not to be used while pregnant—and in

1984 it required a "black box" warning, citing the risk for fetal deformity. A very potent drug indeed.

At the time I took Accutane in 1996, the drug sheets did not say it caused psychosis. Nevertheless, given the timing of when I began taking the drug and the lack of any other possible causes to explain what was going on with me, the sophisticatedly-dressed doctor wondered if my mental status could have been caused by that drug. Perhaps he thought it might have been a side effect, perhaps something more direct, or perhaps he remembered hearing something through the medical grapevine. In any case, he decided it was something to consider.

In 1998, several medical studies cited a possible link between depression and Accutane use. As a result, the FDA issued a warning to physicians, and warning labels in the U.S. were updated to include a possible risk of adverse psychiatric effects, including depression, psychosis, suicidal ideation, and suicide.

By 2002, twenty years after Accutane was released on the market, the FDA Adverse Event Reporting System contained almost twenty-three thousand reports for Accutane, mostly from the U.S. One of the top five most frequent reactions was depression. That year, the drug company Hoffman La-Roche reprinted the drug sheets to state that Accutane was known to cause psychosis.

I often look back on that time and think about the desperate measures we go through to help our self-esteem. Is it always worth it? If somebody told you, "Your acne should clear up, but you might go psychotic on this medication," would you risk it? Of course, when I took the drug, I didn't know its potential impact, and I can't help but wonder if my life might have taken a different path if I hadn't been prescribed Accutane.

CHAPTER 6

Diagnosed Atypical Bipolar

In June 1996, after the initial consultation with the sophisticatedly-dressed doctor, I was hospitalized in an adolescent psychiatric ward. I was seventeen years old. My hair was long and had bleach blonde highlights, courtesy of my hairdresser. My eyes were extra green and had a definite dark green line outlining the pupil from the coloured contacts my optometrist insisted I didn't need. My make-up was unnoticeable. I was innocent and my wardrobe was careless. I often wore my dad's jeans and my black and tan Guess running shoes with thick tan laces.

I stayed on the ward for two and a half months. They diagnosed me as "atypical bipolar," which means after my mania subsides I am still in a psychosis. Essentially, I went from manic with elevated moods into a psychosis for six weeks and then back to base-line—all of which was considered atypical.

Understanding Bipolar

What does the word bipolar actually mean? A literal translation is "two poles." According to the National Institute of Mental Health, "bipolar is a brain disorder that causes unusual shifts in mood, energy, activity levels, and the ability to carry out day-to-day tasks." Bipolar highs are referred to as mania and the lows are depression.

It can be complicated to fully understand, and I am loathe to fill up this book with too much technical information, partly because I am not a medical professional, but also because the field of mental health is always changing due to new information, new treatments, and new diagnoses and language. However, if you think of it from the perspective of someone who has bipolar, it does, in fact, mean two things. Firstly, my brain does not function properly and can sometimes go astray. This happens when my thoughts and emotions are so impaired that my mind goes to a different place with a different reality that is or isn't at all connected to actual reality. Secondly, I have a chemical imbalance that can sometimes lead to emotional pain and irrational conclusions. When this happens, I say that my mind is off-balance.

Bipolar disorder is a mental health condition where periods of depression, mania, or both can occur. Mania or being manic can include feeling euphoria, having high-flown energy, being irritable, being uncooperative, having delusions and or hallucinations, and being over-stimulated. Individuals who experience mania can have trouble finishing a task, have poor concentration, struggle at work, become highly sexual, go on a spending spree, and/or consume significant amounts of drugs or alcohol. According to the American Psychiatric

Association's Diagnostic and Statistical Manual of Mental Disorders (DSM 5, 2013) that psychiatrists in Canada use to evaluate an individual, neither psychosis nor a major depressive episode is a requirement for an individual to be classified as bipolar (p.123). There are several different classifications for bipolar. I was diagnosed as "atypical bipolar." I thought it was because I never went into a depression after a manic phase but it was actually because after my mania subsides I remain in a psychosis for a longer duration. Most individuals who have bipolar go from mania to depression–from highs to lows.

According to the National Institute of Mental Health there are four basic types of bipolar disorder:

- **Bipolar I Disorder**– defined by manic episodes that last at least 7 days or are so severe that the person needs immediate hospital care. Usually, depressive episodes occur as well, typically lasting at least 2 weeks. Episodes of depression with mixed (having depression and manic symptoms at the same time) are also possible.
- **Bipolar II**– defined by patterns of depressive episodes and hypomanic episodes, but not the full-blown manic episodes described above.
- **Cyclothymic Disorder (also called cyclothymia)**– defined by numerous periods of hypomanic symptoms as well numerous periods of depressive symptoms lasting at least 2 years (1 year in children and adolescents). However, the symptoms do not meet the diagnostic requirements for a hypomanic episode and a depressive episode.

- **Other Specified and Unspecified Bipolar and Related Disorders**— defined by bipolar disorder symptoms that do not match the three categories listed above.

Every bipolar individual is different in their moods, episodes, and medications. I would fall under the unspecified bipolar and related disorders category.

To be honest, I hate saying I have bipolar because it is still a faux pas in society and many people are afraid of anyone with any kind of mental illness.

In the years since I was first diagnosed, and more recently while my editor was working on my book, I read many articles and pages of diagnostic manuals and websites, and I also talked with my psychiatrist and other professionals in the community who deal with bipolar in their occupation. What I discovered is that some of what I had been told and what I had heard was incorrect. Much of what I found out was perplexing, as there were so many ambiguous classifications to the illness. Two of the diagnostic manuals differ in the number of classifications, and depending on which organization's manual or which website you search, they all differ in classifying bipolar. Why can't there be one mental health diagnostic manual that is used worldwide?

When my current psychiatrist said there is no such thing as atypical bipolar, I asked him, "What about the NOS (Not Otherwise Specified) category?"

He responded, "That category is only really used when you are first diagnosing someone and you don't have all their details." He then diagnosed me as having schizoaffective disorder because that terminology now appears in the manual, and then he tried to tell me that schizoaffective is the new term for atypical and he can't change my diagnosis. My first psychiatrist diagnosed me as atypical and was careful not to use the word schizoaffective. He had another psychiatrist evaluate me when I was ill and that psychiatrist also said I was atypical. Confusing, to say the least.

I searched high and low for the atypical diagnosis and finally found it in the DSM III (Diagnostic and Statistical Manual of Mental Disorders, 1980). That diagnosis is for someone who doesn't fit into the other categories, which I didn't. By the time DSM IV came out in 2000, the atypical category was gone. So, yes, there once was an atypical bipolar category, but apparently not now.

I was determined to read more and delve further into bipolar. When I finally came across the terminology "unipolar mania," trumpets went off. This diagnosis is not talked about, just like the "lost" atypical diagnosis. Generally, individuals with unipolar mania are lumped in with bipolar, but I know from my experience that it is, in fact, very different, because I never had the ups and downs of bipolar.

Individuals with unipolar mania experience:

- more grandiosity
- more psychotic symptoms—having special powers, such as believing I was a medicine woman
- tendency for excessive energy—when I tumbled down the hallway of the psychiatric ward
- positivity and enthusiasm—when I was ill and was first asked how I was, and I said, "Ecstatic."
- less likely to be suicidal—I was never suicidal, but I was sick and tired of constantly being asked when I was

in the hospital if I *was* suicidal. In order to stop them from asking me, I finally told them, "No, I like myself too much."

- less likely to have co-existing anxiety—I never had co-existing anxiety when I was manic. I only had it after jail. While writing this memoir I figured out that all my anxiety came from everything that happened to me while I was in jail. I was prescribed anti-anxiety pills for a while, but eventually I stopped taking them and haven't suffered with anxiety since.
- less social and work disability—I have maintained life-long friendships, had a number of occupations, including my current job where I am employed full-time, and have a wonderful relationship with everyone in my family.

I realize that with all this information, I am getting a bit ahead of my story, and telling you things that haven't happened yet. But I felt it was important to take a moment and give you some idea of what bipolar is, what it means to me, and how it affects my life.

In any case, I will close this chapter with three recommendations based on my opinion and experience. Firstly, unipolar mania needs to be re-examined, as it has been around since 1899. Secondly, the terminology "unipolar mania" needs to be considered for the next DSM. And finally, it would really help everyone if all the mental health diagnostic manuals were harmonized.

CHAPTER 7

Mental Health Tour

During my hospital stay at age seventeen, my mind was astray and in a psychosis. That was when my thoughts and emotions became so impaired that I lost contact with reality. My mind created a completely new and different story from what had actually happened recently in my life. It told me that my friends and I would be going on tour doing skits and shows about self-esteem, safe sex, and other teen issues, including the story of my friend Andrew's attempted suicide. These shows would be done in schools and other places. My mind had even gone so far as to think that my friends, who would participate in the shows, were going to get new cars and all sorts of other sponsorship.

One day, I picked up the receiver of the tan telephone from a booth on the ward and dialed my friend Larissa. Because my mind thought she would be performing in the show with us, I said to her, "You are going to get a new car." Shortly after, when she came to visit me in the hospital, she said something a little bit surprising. "How did you know I was going to get a new car?" I smiled, but didn't tell her the real reason or the theatrics behind it. Definitely an interesting coincidence.

Making the Psychiatrist's Jaw Drop

The first time the psychiatrist met me my mind was busy working on the theatrics for the show on teen issues. My feet were planted on the carpet at one end of the hall, and I wore my favourite dress. The dress fit my body nicely on the top and was flowy at the waist. My hair hung freely over my shoulders.

At the end of the hall I could see a man I didn't know, and thought he was there to help me with the show. *Performance, theatrics, gymnastics, here I come*. Down the hall my body quickly tumbled back and forth doing gymnastics in my red dress; I successfully completed a round off and three back handsprings. I thought it was such a grand entrance for the show.

My psychiatrist had never seen anything like that before on the psychiatric ward. His mouth hung open for a while, even after I arrived right in front of him. To this day he still talks about how we met—me in my red dress flipping through the air when my mind was astray. He was about six foot two and in his thirties, and had dark blonde hair and thin wire-framed glasses. He always dressed professionally and had nice shoes. Every morning during the week, he ran a group in a room across from the nursing station.

Anosognosia

When my mind goes astray, I do not believe I am ill. This is called anosognosia or "lack of insight," which means I am unaware of the existence of my illness. I couldn't even fathom being ill, and why would I? My grades at school were good, I played basketball, volleyball, field hockey, and soccer, and I ran track. I played piano and trumpet, studied written music, and wrote Royal Conservatory music exams with high marks. I even worked part-time jobs while I was in high school and spent time with friends. And I never drank, smoked, or did drugs. None of these were the accomplishments of someone with a mental illness.

Because I was unaware of the existence of my illness, I refused to take my medications. The only way they could get any medication into me was by injecting it into my butt cheek muscle. Every night it was the same thing. It took four people to medicate me—usually several nurses or nurses' aides and someone from hospital security—with one person holding each arm and one holding each leg. I learned very quickly how to make my body weight as heavy as I could so it would be a struggle for them to carry me. Tears would stream down my face as my arms and legs flailed. It was quite a scene. My mind hated my medication.

During the time I was on the psych ward, I was on two different medications at a time—a mood stabilizer and an antipsychotic. Some of the medications I remember were the antipsychotics Haloperidol, Olanzapine, and Risperidone, and the mood stabilizer Divalproex. All had side effects, but Risperidone was the worst. I couldn't tolerate that one at all and it led to an oculogyric crisis.

The list of medications taken during my illness is staggering. And possibly the direct result of that initial prescription of Accutane, the acne isotretinoin I was given back in 1996.

Tour Selection

The television room on the ward had ugly greeny-blue furniture and drab-looking curtains. Most days one of the patients would switch the channel to MTV and music videos would play. As I watched, I thought I was supposed to select musicians and dancers to go on the "Mental Health Tour" with me to help intrigue the audiences. Maxi Priest featuring Shaggy "That Girl" came on the television. Instantly, my body flowed to the beats of the music because I knew a few lyrics to other Shaggy songs. Shaggy was definitely on the tour. Then another hip hop song came on the television "Only You" by 112 featuring The Notorious B.I.G. and Mase. I knew the lyrics to that song and wasn't afraid to sing them, especially the rap part. It was obvious "Only You" was showcasing the type of dancers who could travel the world with us on the "Mental Health Tour."

At one point, when I was thinking about Andrew's attempted suicide, I went to my room and sat at the desk beside the wall and wrote a poem with him in it. There I called him "d'boy who was disturbed." Right after that, I took a right out of the room headed down the hall, turned left because the ward was rectangular shaped and walked back into the TV room. I heard Jewel on the television and instantly connected with her. I knew she would also be on the tour with us. As more artists were added, my mind said the tour would be a success, but I was the only one who knew about the tour. I never told anyone about it.

Medication Orally

My dad is five foot seven with a medium build, has blue eyes and short greyish hair, and can see distances no problem, but he does need reading glasses. He has a rough exterior, and in high school my friends thought he was in the army by the way he answered the phone. My dad knew I needed to take my medication orally and he wanted to find a way to make it easier for me. He had an idea for my general practitioner.

"Can you type a letter saying that Sandra needs to take her medication orally?"

My G.P. duly typed the letter and Dad brought it to the hospital, where it ended up attached to my chart. For some reason after I was told about that letter, I listened and complied, taking my medication orally without the need for any restraint.

A Mother's Intuition

Side effects of psychiatric medications have caused me much pain in my life. The worst side effect happened one morning when my mom came to see me on the ward. She took one look at me and told the substitute nurse, "Sandra really doesn't look well."

The combination of her work as a nurse and her intuition as a mother meant she was always empathetic and understanding and usually the first to know when I was ill.

"Sandra doesn't look well, don't you think?"

The nurse dismissed Mom's concern. "Sandra is fine and she had a good morning."

"But I'm not sure she looks well at all."

Not able to convince the nurse otherwise, Mom reluctantly left for work.

Less than an hour later, I was lying face down on the carpet in a hallway close to my room. My tongue was hanging out of my mouth and my eyes rolling back into my head. I couldn't move, couldn't put my tongue back in, and had no control over my body movements. That I was fully aware of everything happening to me was terrifying and I was scared beyond belief. They gave me an injection in the rear end, and after about half an hour, my tongue went back into my mouth and my eyes returned to normal. A very frightening experience.

Later they told me I'd had an oculogyric crisis—a reaction to the medication Risperidone—and what a crisis it was.

Every time there was a crisis, the patients on the ward would discuss it during group. My sharply dressed doctor came in every morning and threw his suit jacket and tie in the corner. One day, when they allowed me to have a pass, I wore one of my dad's old suit jackets and ties to group and mimicked my doctor by walking in the room and taking off my jacket and tie just as he did. He liked the joke.

During group or on the ward I always wanted to help other patients who were not doing well. When they would swear, I encouraged them to use other words. My biggest success was a young patient around eleven years old who had an eating disorder and was afraid to swallow any food at all. When I asked her what she *would* eat, she exclaimed, "Ice cream." I told my parents and asked if they would bring some ice cream with them the next time they came to the ward. That ended up being a very good idea because the patient with the eating disorder finally ate and wasn't afraid to swallow the ice cream or even any other food after that.

Trying to Escape

I always wanted to escape from the ward because it made me feel like I was in jail. Not that I knew what being in jail was like, but I just needed a way out and knew that others felt the same. So, one afternoon I tried running out of the ward, but that attempt was foiled by one of the nurses, who barrelled me down at the door. She was the largest female nurse there. That was not a good feeling, emotionally or physically. I knew there was no getting out of there, but in my mind I had to try.

During one meeting with the doctor, I talked casually about getting out of the ward. "I'd like your keys and pass." *That will allow me to come and go as I please.*

The doctor looked at me through his glasses. "No."

My green eyes looked at him as I said, "Well then, I'd like an independent pass."

The well-put-together psychiatrist answered, "That'd be like giving you my keys *and* pass."

He never gave me either, but one evening I discovered the quiet room where they locked patients in to scream and holler. They had left the door open, and I wandered in. Soon I noticed the exciting echo in there. I immediately started singing. From then on, every night the nurses would unlock the quiet room so I could sing. Singing was therapeutic and it made me feel wonderful.

Friends and Family

Every day during my hospitalization I used the phone. Being able to connect with people outside made me feel good. The phone was in my hands the instant it became available. I called my friends and asked them to come and visit me, and they did. During one of my parents' visits, one of the nurses told them, "If Sandra keeps calling people, she'll soon have no friends at all." Later, she called my parents to apologize for what she had said. Her excuse? She was trying to quit smoking.

Mom told me that story much later when I was in a healthier mindset. At the time, however, I thought that was so rude of her. In any case, she was completely wrong. None of my friends in high school ever left me because of my illness.

While I was on the psych ward, a lot of friends from high school, both male and female, came to visit me in the hospital, and when I went back to school, they didn't treat me like an outcast or stop being friends with me. I did grow apart from many of them after leaving school, but doesn't that happen to a lot of us? And when I was hospitalized in my thirties, friends often phoned my parents' house to find out where I was. My parents never gave them too much information because I wouldn't allow it: "You can't tell them anything." I'm sure some of them may have possibly felt confused about why they hadn't seen me and why I hadn't been in contact with them, and there were a few people later on who couldn't handle me having bipolar, including one person who refused to believe I even had bipolar, despite all the evidence to the contrary. But other than that, nobody I knew left me at any point in time when I was ill. Even if I couldn't talk to them while I was ill, we always talked afterward and made up.

My parents visited me on the ward every day and my brother visited as often as he could. In fact, the family support I received whenever I was ill is one of the reasons I have been so successful in my life. They talked to me when I needed to talk, both in person and over the telephone. Without my family I would not be where I am today. When I was manic, I told them they couldn't come to see me on the ward. They understood and left me alone for a couple of days, but eventually they came back.

Their visits and unconditional support when I was mentally ill were integral to my wellness, as it is for any individual who is mentally ill. But not everyone with a mental illness has that. I know I am lucky, and I am grateful beyond words.

I Want to Act

My parents would have let me pursue acting if I had just said the magic words, "I want to act." But I never did. The first time I admitted to myself that I wanted to act was during that hospitalization in 1996. Whenever I watched television shows growing up, I wanted the job of the actresses on the series. It wasn't until I hit the hospital ward, did gymnastics on my way to meeting my psychiatrist, participated in music therapy, sang in the quiet room, and, at the behest of the psychiatrist, "write a script about being on the ward with everyone in group" that I fully realized performing was embedded in my bones.

The Importance of Writing

Shortly after grade eight, my parents showed me the importance of writing things down to record what people said when they didn't treat me fairly. While I was in hospital, however, I took that up a notch. I began to journal my experiences and thoughts about my illness, and wrote poems about what I was feeling at various times. Later on, I journaled on trips and while travelling, and I also learned to free-write at university. I wanted to express myself and record the many things, good and bad, that happened to me, but it became more than that. It was an important record of who I am and what I went through. And because I kept a lot of what I wrote, I have been able to use my writing to tell my story in even greater detail than I can remember. I'm not sure I really knew how important all that writing was at the time, but I am grateful for every word.

CHAPTER 8

You Will Never Succeed

In late August when I was finally discharged from the ward, a few of the healthcare professionals I dealt with wanted me to finish high school in a small specialized school. I said no and went back to my high school in September. I was determined to succeed, but there was a major obstacle in the way. After my discharge, my psychiatrist arranged for me to be tested by a psychologist. He did a few tests, including a Rorschach test where you describe what you see in the inkblots. I learned the hard way that you definitely cannot be creative in your answers. The psychologist thought I was an idiot and told me I would never finish high school. That made me feel unintelligent, and I decided to prove him wrong.

Back in high school in time for my grade twelve year, being on student council turned out to be a blessing in disguise. Because my medications made me so incredibly tired, every day during my spare period I would go into the Student Council room, flick the light switch off, lock the door, and sleep. Because of the medications I was on, I was so bagged that I needed to sleep eighteen hours a day.

Medications were not my friends. I was put on different types in combination, always an antipsychotic with a mood stabilizer—Haloperidol and Depakote, Risperidone and Depakote, Olanzapine and Depakote, and Olanzapine and Lithium—until they found one that worked for me. Every patient is different in what works for them.

Whatever they tried, the side effects were always nasty. The mood-stabilizer Depakote caused so much of my hair to thin and fall out in large clumps that my mom actually came to my session to tell my psychiatrist how bad it was. After discussion he took me off that drug and put me on Lithium. When the antipsychotic medication Haloperidol left a metallic taste in my mouth, the doctor tried Olanzapine, but that caused me to gain forty pounds, which rocked my self-esteem to the utter core. Forty pounds—one third of my body weight at that time, weight that did not come off easily. I nicknamed that medication "the fat drug."

When I asked my psychiatrist if there was anything I could do about the weight gain, he suggested taking Metformin (a drug for diabetes) to suppress my appetite, plus hard cardio. "And make sure you sweat a lot." He was athletic, and knew what he was talking about; he also knew I needed a kick in the pants to really get going. And get going I did, although shedding the weight was painful and proved to be no easy task. Still, I stuck with it, the words of my psychiatrist ringing in my ears all the way.

The cardio definitely helped, but eventually I also made the decision to modify my diet. I'd heard that diet is seventy to eighty per cent of successful weight loss, so I stopped eating after dinner, only ate one dessert a day, and replaced juice with water. Those modifications alone saw me drop ten pounds in two weeks.

Much of grade twelve had been spent in bed. I tried out for the basketball team, but was too exhausted to play. I was too slow, weighed too much, was too lethargic, and had lost a lot of hair. There was no quality of life at all. So in late February 1997, after six months of taking psychiatric medications, I decided to go off them—with the permission of my psychiatrist. Life normalized again. I could live and breathe and there was no more being trapped in zombie land.

Even though I struggled during that year with all those side effects, my perseverance and determination paid off. I finished high school the way I wanted.

Accutane Strikes Again

Unfortunately, the decision to go off my medication turned into a nightmare. One day in July I found some leftover Accutane pills on the top shelf in the kitchen cupboard at my house where it was stored with Tylenol and other medication. I took the Accutane to my room and for some reason popped them in my mouth and swallowed them down. I hid the rest of the pills in the top drawer of my white dresser and self-administered as I saw fit. Who knows if that was the real reason for my onset, but there was my mental illness putting me back in the hospital again, back on the same ward, back with the same psychiatrist.

On November 4, 1997, after three months of hospitalization, I was finally discharged. While I had graduated with enough credits, I didn't have enough of the correct credits to enter university. So in January 1998, I went back to high school to finish one more credit. I wanted to take psychology, but Mom suggested I take law, and I compromised by signing up for both. I thought I would love psychology because of what I had been through, but it didn't relate to my illness the way I wanted. I eventually dropped that subject and only completed law. I loved law, and still have the notebook from that course.

During that time, I was prescribed many medications and struggled with their side effects. Once again, I had no quality of life and no social life. Lithium made me feel terrible and caused me to sleep eighteen hours a day.

I was also on Quetiapine, which caused stiffness to my whole body. That was the worst side effect and would not go away. My wrists were cogwheeling and stiff when the psychiatrist tested them. So then I was put on Benzatropine (Cogentin) to mask the stiffness, but that caused me to have severe blurred vision to the point that I couldn't drive. My psychiatrist had the pharmacist cut the 25mg Quetiapine tablet down into smaller and smaller doses to mitigate the stiffness. By the time it was cut into one-sixteenth, the pharmacist finally gave up "You might as well sniff the medication." Clearly, such a small dose would have no effect, and my psychiatrist took me off it completely.

Trying to understand my atypical bipolar was difficult. A lot of medications and dosages were tried and the side effects were many and confusing and difficult to deal with. Overall it was a terrible experience. Before long, I chose to go off the medications because my body could no longer tolerate the sleepiness and the stiffness.

Sheila

My twin friends Melanie and Larissa both had boyfriends and it was harder to get together with them. Instead, I went out dancing with a crowd of other people, one of whom was a girl named Sheila. She had long dark hair and dark eyes. I bumped into her again in a gym one day while I was working for the school division and we chatted. A few months later, after my hospitalization, I looked up Sheila's number in the phone book. I picked up my clear see-through light-up phone and called her to see if she would like to go out. She agreed. We knew the same people, became good friends, and often went out dancing together. After dancing we would discuss our night out over a late-night breakfast.

Every Individual Can Affect You

On January 29, 1998, I was at the hospital waiting to see my psychiatrist. I bumped into a nurse who used to take care of me on the ward and we talked for just a couple of minutes. Then while I was in session with my psychiatrist, she phoned him and said she thought I was going manic. The psychiatrist was surprised by her comment because he could tell I wasn't manic and was, in fact, well, but that judgement on her part really messed with my brain.

I have always believed that every individual you meet can affect you, but what she said that day caused me to start pushing down my feelings. And she wasn't the only one who shook me up and damaged my self-esteem because of what they said about my illness.

A few years after that incident, I was at my brother's wedding when he made the most beautiful speech about me. The words he used to describe me were exactly how I felt about him. I was smiling outside and crying inside, but did not shed a tear. Shortly afterward, my cousin came up to me and announced, "You don't have a heart if you didn't cry at that speech."

Painfully, my illness, my self-esteem, and what that nurse and others said about my illness have all affected my emotions so deeply that to this day I bottle up my emotions and push down my feelings.

CHAPTER 9

Ten Years

After my medications were discontinued in 1998, I was well for the next ten years. During that time, I worked, travelled, studied, and enjoyed being me with my friends and family.

Taekwondo

I enrolled in taekwondo in 1999, and was fully committed to it until 2006, after which I attended classes on and off for another five years. During that time, I met Tatiana, with her long auburn hair and green eyes, and we became good friends.

My taekwondo instructor stood about six foot one and was a five-time world champion. I told Tatiana that taekwondo was like my church. Not so much in the praying department, but in how you were preached at. Everything my instructor said during class had meaning to it and proved to be constant life lessons. It was like he secretly knew what was going on in my life and was talking about it in front of everyone. One time he told us, "People can only bring you down for so long before you have to let them go." At that exact point in my life, I was having trouble with a jealous boyfriend who was bringing me down. *How does he know?*

Somehow my instructor always knew how to make me and everyone feel better. If something wasn't right he could sense it and would give us a pep talk. He would always remind us, "If one door closes, kick another one open," figuratively speaking, of course. Or he'd say, "If a situation happens that you don't like, adapt and overcome it." That was also meant for the fighting ring. If you got kicked in a fight, adapt to it and do something better to the opponent.

Classes were taught in English and Korean. We had written tests at every belt level so we would know the Korean words for counting and the different taekwondo moves, such as *chagi*—kick, *mahki*—block, and *chirugi*—punch. Every class started with a warm-up counting in Korean, followed by kicking and punching. Then it would be a sparring class, a kicking/punching class, or a forms class. At the beginning of each class we lined up in order of our belt rank and stood with our knees bent and shouting (*kihap*) as we punched or kicked to the commands of the instructor.

At times the classes made me feel like I was in the military. We were taught discipline and to respect elders. We had to bow to individuals older than us. My instructor always taught us to think outside the box and to push boundaries. And he challenged us to study different forms of martial arts in other countries.

Slinging Pizza and Pints

In 2001, while attending the University of Winnipeg at the age of twenty-one, I was corporate trained for waitressing and started slinging pizza and pints at Boston Pizza. I met many new friends, which helped my self-esteem.

Emma was about five foot eight, petit, had long brown hair and blue eyes, and studied nursing at university. We became fast friends. We worked together, she in the lounge and me in the restaurant. We undertook fifty hours of volunteer training as body image and self-esteem educators, went to the same university, and went on vacations and through relationships together.

Once while we were away in Mexico, Emma had a few too many drinks and jumped into the pool with her clothes on. We always laughed and had some of the best discussions together.

Maggie was about five feet, very lean with short black hair. She was a bit of a jokester, always fun, liked to make trouble in a good way, and was always making us laugh. Emma, Maggie, and I would often get together and study at either someone's house or at the Salisbury House restaurant on Main Street.

One of my professors at the university said you were very lucky if you had one or two really good friends in your life. Maggie and Emma were mine.

George was a manager at the restaurant and most people liked to work with him because he was very laid back. He was five foot seven, and had blonde curly hair and green eyes. Because he tanned easily, people thought he was from California, but he was clearly Caucasian. He had quite the sense of humour and was always cracking jokes. If you understood his humour you were sure to spend part of your shift chuckling along with him.

Not everyone understood or appreciated George's kind of humour, and sometimes his jokes went right over my head. But one thing I knew was that while all of us were there together, there was much laughter, friendship, and good times at Boston Pizza in Winnipeg.

Accutane Lawsuit

While at home one night in the winter of 2002, I watched a television show about a medical student in Edmonton suing a drug company for ten million dollars. The case was settled out of court, and the company was Hoffman La-Roche, the makers of Accutane—the drug I had been taking for my acne. When I researched the case, I found articles about the lawsuit that really provoked my interest and made me question my own psychiatric hospitalizations. I remembered what the first doctor who saw me in the hospital wrote in my chart—"Query reaction to Accutane"—and wondered again whether that drug might have caused my psychosis.

Then one day some of the staff at Boston Pizza started talking about Accutane. The bartender, who was tall, with brown eyes and dark hair, listened intently to my story and about the lawsuit. He said his sister was a lawyer and worked at a firm that deals with medical lawsuits. He talked to her for me and gave me her contact info the next day.

Two days later, I contacted his sister, and she connected me with a lawyer at her firm who specifically handled those types of cases. I made an appointment to see him and went with my parents to his downtown firm. The lawyer and I met in his office alone. I described my case to him—how I had taken Accutane both times before my two adolescent hospitalizations for psychosis, and what the doctor had written in my chart.

The lawyer looked at me with his eyes squinting. "Do you drink or do drugs?"

"No, I've never drank *or* done drugs."

And that is still the truth. Peer pressure never got to me and I never needed alcohol or drugs to have a good time. Also, my brother Michael doesn't drink and I look up to him because he is a good role model for me.

Besides, my mind knows what it is like to be in a psychosis. That feeling of losing your inhibitions, or your mind, is the worst feeling in the world. I hate it more than anything and I never want to feel mindless again. If other people want to let loose, that's fine. I don't frown upon it. But I have only consumed six alcoholic drinks in my entire life. Getting drunk is *so* not an option for me.

The lawyer pointed at me. "I just don't want to be in the courtroom with my pants dangling around my ankles."

What the fuck does that mean? Does he not believe me? Does he think I'm lying?

That lawyer eventually talked me out of pursuing the case. He thought there was no chance of winning and was afraid of his dick showing in the courtroom. And judging by his words and his manner, he clearly thought I was a liar.

Recently, my mom found and sent me the pamphlets from Hoffman La-Roche that I received when I first went on Accutane. They only talked about mood once—"If there are noticeable changes in your mood you should tell your doctor" (Hoffmann La-Roche, 1988). Now the Accutane drug sheet that comes with the medication states if you take the drug you may experience "signs of mental health problems such as depression or psychosis (a severe mental disturbance)" (Hoffmann La-Roche, 2014). I can tell you that severe mental disturbance and psychosis are *way* different than noticeable changes in your mood.

When I had acne and tried every available prescription and non-prescription medication to get rid of it, it was very difficult for me. My self-esteem and self-image took a beating, and that played on my self-worth. Could I have lived with myself with acne? Probably, although it would have been difficult enough. But if someone had told me, "If you take this medication you could be living in a psychiatric ward and you'll face challenges the rest of your life because of it," I know for sure I would have reconsidered ever taking Accutane. If there was a possibility that my life could have had no mental illness, I would be the first in line to say, "Sign me up."

Muay Thai Kickboxing

For two weeks in March 2002, I was on vacation in Puerto Vallarta, Mexico, with a few friends from Boston Pizza. When I asked around about martial arts classes, one of the activity staff at the hotel told me about a kickboxing class he was taking. I went to that class four times while I was there and fell in love with the way the instructor taught. He pushed you and challenged you, and the classes were in Spanish. The gym was nothing like I had ever seen. It had barbed-wire fences that allowed open air to flow through. That definitely helped with the heat that sometimes caused puddles of sweat due to the intensity of the workout. When I returned to Winnipeg I longed to go back to Puerto Vallarta to train some more.

In May of that year, I packed my bags for California. I was going to see my friend Sheila who had moved there for an accountant job. From California, I planned to make my way to P.V. When I got to Winnipeg Airport, a customs officer asked me how long I planned on being away.

"Eighty-eight days."

"What?" he exclaimed. "Get into that room." He pointed and followed me into a nearby room.

Once I was in the screening room, he began with his questions. "So you're moving to L.A.?"

Calmly I explained, "No, I'm going to visit my friend in California and then I'm going to Mexico."

"So you're moving to L.A.?" he repeated.

"No," I answered.

"Well, how do I know you'll be back?"

"I have school in the fall," I told him.

"School?"

"A photography course at Red River College in Winnipeg, where I live."

He looked intently at me for a moment, and then said, "I'm giving you ninety days and if you're not back by then, we're coming to look for you."

You are ridiculous, I thought. *And this is a terrible way to start my Saturday morning.*

I arrived in California on May 26 and stayed with Sheila for a little over a week before flying to P.V. Once I got there, the Muay Thai kickboxing training was crazy. I had to carry other students on my back, I was kicking and punching on the spot to the sound of a bell going off, kicking target pads, punching bags, and learning a couple of sneaky manoeuvres to deke out my opponents. I definitely exuded sweat from the astounding workouts.

While I was in P.V., I not only learned a lot about myself and another culture, but I also enjoyed my journey of experiencing another form of martial arts in a different country. It was amazing.

A Change of Direction

When I arrived back in Winnipeg in the fall, I found myself wondering why people were so concerned with little things like traffic. Everyone in Mexico had the attitude, "If you miss one bus it doesn't matter because there will be another one in four minutes." I really thought people in Canada needed to relax more.

I lived at home and fully intended to make the most of the photography course I had signed up for at Red River College. But after the first class, I knew it wasn't for me, and decided to drop out.

Later that same week I was at a taekwondo class and my instructor asked me, "What are you doing these days?"

When I told him about the failed photography class, he offered up a few other suggestions for me to consider. "What about nursing? My nurse friend always calls me with interesting stories."

"I don't want to be a nurse." My mom had put up with so much in her nursing career that I wasn't interested.

Then he suggested, “What about nutrition? Then you could help me with all of those diet plans.”

“Hmmmm, that sounds interesting. Maybe.”

That night at home, I thought about what the instructor had suggested. I had always loved learning about food and even won a nutrition award at a divisional science fair when I was younger. It was for a project I did titled “Have you had your water today?” I did experiments on dehydration, water, and foods. A healthy upbringing with proper nutritious meals was always part of my life and I liked learning about nutrition.

Because pharmaceutical sales also interested me, I wondered if a science degree would help me get a career in that industry. Back in 2000, I had written the university entrance exam for pharmacy, but I didn’t get in. Two years later, I realized that if it’s true you get half your occupation from your dad and half from your mom, then I got sales from Dad and science from Mom. All that added up to a possible career in pharmaceutical sales.

I began looking online for information about nutrition courses at the University of Manitoba, and within a week I had enrolled at the Faculty of Human Ecology in the program Human Nutritional Sciences. I wasn’t able to start at university until January 2003, so while I waited I went back to work at Boston Pizza. When I wasn’t working or doing taekwondo, I was hanging out with Emma and Maggie.

The University of Manitoba was a thirty- to forty-five-minute drive from my house, depending on traffic. The first semester of classes I attended went until the end of April. I especially enjoyed the course Foods, Facts, and Fallacies where I learned interesting tidbits such as brick cheddar cheese has more protein than ground beef. During that time,

I continued waitressing, and during the summer break, I attended a week-long taekwondo camp.

Taekwondo Training

My instructor put on one-week camps during the summers that included taekwondo, running, doing hills, and swimming. There were at least six hours of training a day and they were gruelling. Tatiana, two other girls, and I slept in a twelve-by-six coat closet of a community centre for the entire week. We were so tired by the end of each day that it didn't matter where we slept; we just wanted to sleep.

I felt very uncomfortable at that camp because for a while, I wasn't able to go to the restroom. One night when some of us were having drinks on a patio, a guy at least thirty years older than me asked, "How are you doing?" I thought it was inappropriate for him to be hitting on me given the huge age difference. I looked at him and announced, "Not good. I'm constipated."

We did fun activities at night, like attending a Goldeyes baseball game in Winnipeg. Our instructor Carla was training for Nationals at the time and she had to lose weight to be able to make her weight category. While we were at the baseball park Carla started a conversation with the worker at the Boston Pizza kiosk; the two knew each other from school. The worker told Carla they were throwing the leftover pizza out and she was welcome to have some. Because Carla was starved from so much training and barely eating, she snuck out some of the pizza, gnawing it down as quickly as she could. Of course, my instructor's eagle eyes caught her from across the stadium, but strangely he didn't approach her. Instead he left a voicemail on her cell phone. When she let us listen to it, all it said was "Numb, numb, numb" with some chewing noises. We all burst out laughing.

After the Goldeyes game one of the instructors who was driving us back to the community centre stopped at the drug store for me. Everyone knew about my restroom issues – no secrets in camp. The pharmacist I spoke to suggested I take both a stool softener and Senokot, a laxative that can sometimes cause you to run to the toilet. I bought a box of each and we headed back to the community centre.

The next morning we drove to a school and ran straight out onto their sports field. I snuck into the school because I had to use the washroom. Everyone noticed I was gone for at least twenty minutes, maybe half an hour. When I came back outside everyone cheered for me, so I put my hands straight up in the air like it was a victory and I was on a podium receiving a gold medal. It was a victory, of sorts. The relief was amazing.

That night back at the community centre, we were relaxing after kicking and exercising all day. Carla told me she was having trouble going to the washroom and wanted to take the constipation pills I had.

"Which one?" I asked.

"Senokot."

When I gave her one of those pills, she grabbed some water and threw it back.

Some of the other students were watching a movie while Carla, Tatiana, and I spent the rest of the night talking about the training and our day.

The next morning we had breakfast early and headed to the pool. The kicking against the weight of the water helped strengthen our taekwondo kicks. Before I entered the pool I had to use the toilet because the constipation pills were by then in full force. Then out of nowhere I heard this *Bang, Bang, Bang, Bang* on the door of the metal stall right next to me. *What the heck?* I thought.

Then I heard Carla yelling. "Get the hell out of the stall. Get the hell out of the stall."

When I finally got out of my stall, I saw Carla washing her hands. "Who were you yelling at?"

She replied, "I had to go to the toilet so bad and some lady wouldn't get out of the stall."

I burst out laughing. "You were asking a stranger to get the hell out of the stall?"

"Yes," she giggled. "I had to go so bad. Damn Senokot."

We both laughed.

Tournaments

Taekwondo tournaments were a time to battle and compete. We were taught to be warriors. Our instructor's motto was "Our strength is our spirit." Winning a fight wasn't always about the hardest kicks; it was also about strategy. I did very well in tournaments and won most of the ones I entered. I was very flexible from my gymnastics days and my favourite kick was the axe kick. I would kick straight up about six feet in the air and come down like an axe with my heel. Another of my favourites was the crescent kick, which is another high section kick. During tournaments, girls would swing at me with their fists because of my high kicks. But that is illegal in tournaments, and whenever they did it, the fight was stopped. Another time a girl sat down on a chair and wouldn't get back up because she was afraid of my kicks. I loved to compete, and the thrill of competing was always exciting for me.

In December 2005 I completed my Bachelor of Science in Nutrition from the University of Manitoba. Five courses are considered a full load at university, but in order to finish the degree half a semester early, I did six courses in one of the terms. I wanted to finish early and not have to go back for one last course the next year. Going from one assignment to the next was hectic and extremely intense, but I made it through. During that year at university, I also volunteered as a facilitator for body image and self-esteem sessions, as well as at the hospital with a dietitian working on nutrition projects. I even applied for a one-year internship with Dietitians of Canada. The three programs I applied for ran for thirty-five to forty weeks and provided opportunities for individuals to train in hospitals or other facilities. With a total of sixteen spots between the three programs I applied to I was hopeful I would get in.

In January 2006, four of us were training for Nationals. Tatiana and I trained together with a male blackbelt, while Carla trained on her own. Our days were spent swimming, running, or doing hills early in the morning before work, followed by intense two-hour classes at night. We battled and fought at night time, women against men. We learned mental toughness, and often got bruises, but that was all part of how we trained and improved.

My black belt test was in 2006. It was intense and difficult, and a gruelling experience overall. Sweat dripped off my forehead and tears of effort ran from my eyes. I had to break at least twelve boards, grapple, spar with three people coming at me at once, do many patterns—one for each belt level—punch and kick, and write a Korean word test. After it was over, Carla told me, “My mom said that he really gave it to you out there.” Yes, he did, but at the time I didn’t really notice. I was too focused on making it through each moment and doing whatever I could to earn my black belt.

Territory Manager

I still waitressed at Boston Pizza, but regularly looked at the classifieds for a different job. One Saturday I came across an interesting opportunity as a Territory Manager in the consumer packaged goods industry selling cookies, crackers, and candy. The position was a one-year term. I immediately applied and landed an interview soon afterward.

The same week as the interview for the cookie selling job, a few things happened that took me on a bit of a rollercoaster ride. A girl I knew from university emailed me with the message, “Congratulations on the dietetic internship.” When I emailed her back to find out how she knew I got an internship, she admitted that she didn’t actually know, she just assumed. That really got my hopes up, so a few days later when the letter arrived about the internship, I was very excited—until I opened it and saw I had been completely rejected. *Why did she have to say that to me? This really hurts.* Unfortunately for me, the rejection letter arrived the same day I had to go for the consumer packaged goods interview. I wasn’t sure I could sit through that entire interview with a forced smile on my face.

The man who interviewed me was friendly, forthcoming, and down-to-earth. There were two interviews—one with him alone, and one with him and his boss—and they seemed interested in hiring me. When they told me I got the job, I was very excited. *Sometimes when something bad happens, something better* does *come along.* I only said I would take the position if they gave me time off to compete at taekwondo Nationals in May. When they agreed to that, I was even happier.

My job came with a van and I was hired to start work the first week of April. On the morning of April 1 as I was reaching for my cereal, my dad said to me, "Your boss called and he wants to know what kind of a cookie you want on the side of the van. A chocolate chip cookie or one with sprinkles?" Half asleep I looked at him in disbelief. He kept going on about the cookie and the van until he finally admitted, "April Fool!" *Not funny, Dad.*

As a Territory Manager, my job was to drive around the city and surrounding areas, take my computer into grocery stores and big box stores, write orders, and up-sell displays to increase incremental sales. I was trained for one week by the two other Territory Managers who worked for the company, and they taught me a lot of the ins and outs of the job. There were many interactions every day with multiple people in the stores as well as the customers who were shopping there. Some people were real characters.

In May 2006 we went to taekwondo Nationals in Halifax, Nova Scotia. That was the first time I had to drop weight, and it nearly killed me. I had to be 121 pounds or under, but by the time I arrived in Halifax two days prior to the tournament, I was still 125 pounds. I tried running it off, but that was a mistake because it hardly made any difference and completely exhausted me. The only way I could lose the weight was to sweat off as much as possible in the sauna, with Tatiana as my spotter. I also sucked on lemons instead of eating.

The pressure to make-weight was unlike anything I'd ever experienced before. By the time the tournament began, I weighed in at 119 pounds, but unfortunately, my body was way too exhausted and I didn't perform as well as I wanted. Still, I was happy to have had the experience.

Tatiana and I were still eager to compete after Nationals, and because of my gymnastics background, I had suggested doing bodybuilding/fitness competitions. In the fall, Tatiana went to a meeting about that and decided it was definitely for us. I trained for fitness and Tatiana trained for figures. Our five-days-a-week workouts consisted of weights for one to two hours with a specific diet plan. Saturdays we practised posing in our swimsuits and heels so we would be able to pose on stage for the competitions. Twice a week I went to gymnastics classes, and after the initial bulking-up period to gain muscle mass, we added about two to four hours of cardio to our day to lean out. We were only supposed to bike or walk to keep our buttocks round, but because the weight wouldn't come off me, I ran as well. My trainer never knew; he just said I looked good.

I trained for three competitions. My theme and outfit for the gymnastics portion was *Kill Bill*. I placed second at novice and provincials in Manitoba, and third at the World Qualifiers in Toronto. Nobody else at the gym where I trained did World Qualifiers, and I was very pleased with my results.

After the competitions I went to the Calgary Stampede. After seeing the rodeo, I decided I wanted a new challenge. I told my trainer I wanted to go into bull riding because there were no women in that field, but he said it would be too hard on my body. Initially, I was disappointed, but when he told me a guy at the gym had asked that his appointment be booked at the same time as mine because of how I motivated people, well, that really made me smile.

CHAPTER 10

Job with a Car

My contract in Winnipeg as a Territory Manager finished in May 2007. I immediately started to study for the GMAT—Graduate Management Admission Test—because I was interested in pursuing a Master of Business Administration (MBA). You had to pass that test to get into an MBA program. I found a course in Ontario that would help me prepare for the GMAT, and in the summer, I flew to Toronto and stayed with my Aunt Kay and Uncle Gerald in the suburb of Oakville.

Shortly after arriving, I stayed overnight with a high school friend who lived in the downtown area. After walking the forty-five minutes from my friend's house to the University of Toronto, I knew the downtown was where I wanted to live. The vibrancy and energy of the city felt right, and although it looked a bit like a concrete jungle, I felt quite at home there.

My parents had always helped me with anything I needed, and they were very supportive of the move. We packed my belongings into my dad's green Pontiac and drove from Winnipeg to Toronto. I didn't take my car because I had already decided, "I'm going to get a job with a car."

The real estate market was so competitive that it was difficult to find a place to rent. After a week of searching with no luck, one of my cousins who also lived downtown recommended a realtor to help.

The realtor told us about a few condos that were available. The first one we saw was very dirty and I decided I wasn't interested, but when we looked at it again a few days later, we all agreed it just needed a good cleaning. Realizing the place could look better with a bit of elbow grease, and given there wasn't anything else suitable for me, I signed the agreement and rented the suite.

The condo was at the corner of Fort York Boulevard and Bathurst Street. My suite was on the twelfth floor and had a beautiful view of the water. A mere ten-minute walk away was King Street, hot yoga, a grocery store, a drug store, a coffee shop, a sword class, an acting class, and public transportation. For the first couple of months, I had free Internet access because someone in the building hadn't locked their WiFi. Even though I could only access it from the tiny den area of my suite, I wasn't going to complain.

The free WiFi allowed me to send out job applications and acting/stunt resumes. When I emailed my old boss in Winnipeg to ask if he could be a reference for me, I was sure he would say yes. He was a wonderful boss, caring, kind-hearted, and made you want to work hard every day and be successful at what you did. Not only did he agree, but he also told me the consumer packaged goods company I worked for in Winnipeg was hiring in Toronto. A chance to get my old cookie selling job back, except in a larger city.

When I told my aunt and uncle about the possible job, Aunt Kay said, "Oh, like a Girl Scout?"

"No," I replied proudly. "Like a Territory Manager."

Cookies and a Map

I emailed the District Manager at the Toronto office, and he quickly followed up with a phone interview. Because that went well, and given my old boss was a reference, I was invited to attend an in-person interview with both the District Manager and the Director of Sales Execution. I wasn't nervous for either interview because I had done the job before and knew exactly what to expect.

I wasn't surprised to be offered the position of Territory Manager, but I was extremely proud of myself—and also very happy because the job came with a company car, just like I said it would. I was handed a thick book with all sorts of maps and addresses of the grocery stores in my area, which was mostly downtown Toronto. I didn't have GPS at the time, so that book became my best friend. I studied it and figured out the best way to drive to my destinations. Navigating the city was initially a challenge after the relative ease and familiarity of Winnipeg, but I learned very quickly to avoid the chaos of busy streets such as Bloor Street.

Dream Role

Shortly after starting my new job, I received an email response to one of the resumes I'd sent out for an acting part. They wanted me to audition for a superhero movie that included stunt work. That was a dream role for me. Back handsprings, kicks, and dive rolls were just some of the moves I did for the audition. When I landed the lead role in that film, I was on top of the moon. Unfortunately, the project never went anywhere, but I was hopeful it would lead to other opportunities.

Karen

One of my childhood friends also lived in Toronto. Karen and I went to elementary and junior high school together, and used to choreograph gymnastics routines on my parents' lawn. She had waist-length black hair and blue eyes, and lived a twenty-minute walk from my condo. She moved to Toronto to work as an engineer and loved Pad Thai. I was lucky to have her as a friend in Toronto. We had fun going out together and she helped me feel less lonely. Through Karen, I met an Irish girl named Lindsay who also worked as an engineer. Her hair was thick and her accent adorable. The three of us went out on the weekends, sometimes with other people and sometimes just by ourselves. More often than not, we ended up dancing at Brant House on King Street.

Dreaming about Orlando

One November weekend prior to a visit from my friend Tatiana from Winnipeg, I was out on King Street at a lounge with Karen and Lindsay. When I finally walked home it was about 1:00 a.m. I wasn't afraid to walk by myself late at night because I had my black belt in taekwondo. That night, I was wearing my high Guess boots that were one size too big; they were the last pair on sale and I just had to buy them. My feet clopped down the street because even though I used an insert to make the boots fit better, they were still awkward to walk in.

When I made a right on Front Street, I could see a small limo bus stopped up ahead on the corner of that street and Bathurst. *Pirates of the Caribbean* was playing on the huge screen television in the front of the vehicle. Why I stood there and watched the movie, I'll never know, but that night when my head hit the pillow I dreamt I met Orlando Bloom in a bar. The next morning I journaled about my dream.

Tatiana and Training

Since 2006, Tatiana and I had trained together, competed together, and helped each other do what we needed to achieve our goals. In those two years, we trained more than most people do in a lifetime. Whenever we were together, we always had the best time and were strong supports for each other. And because we had been through so much together, we had become great friends. I was very excited she was coming to Toronto to visit me.

Every weekend I used to walk for ten minutes to buy a copy of the *Toronto Star*. Why? So I could read Phil Booth's horoscopes, of course. It was an indulgent purchase, but one I enjoyed doing. When Tatiana came to visit, I skipped that indulgent purchase completely. I was happy she was there, and didn't need any horoscope to tell me that.

Dreams Come True

The Friday night Tatiana arrived, we went to a pub on King Street. I had invited Karen and Lindsay to join us, but they both declined. After we finished at the pub, we walked outside. The snow was gently falling and it all looked rather pretty.

We were deciding where to go next when we met a French guy. He asked us where we were going, and then started toward Brant House, which was a ways down the street, as if he assumed we would simply follow him. Then my eyes caught sight of a canopy above a door much closer to where we were standing.

"I want to go here," I exclaimed, pointing up at the canopy to the Century Room.

Tatiana looked at the French guy and also pointed up. "We're going here."

He hurried back and told us to stand in the VIP line. Tatiana and I whispered back and forth; we didn't want or need him to get us in.

But the French guy insisted. "It's okay. I will take care of it."

Then he greased the bouncer so the three of us could get in ahead of everyone else still standing in line. Once inside the front door, we found out he had no more money and needed us to pay his $20 cover.

As soon as we stepped in the bar, I looked up, pleasantly surprised to see Orlando Bloom. Tatiana was shocked.

The guy he was with pointed at Orlando and said to me, "Look, it's Orlando Bloom."

I looked at him with my green eyes and declared, "I know. He's beautiful."

Later that evening Orlando was off in a corner close to where we were. He was standing with his back to us, so I approached him and tapped him on the shoulder. He slowly, very slowly, turned around to face me. As my eyes looked into his, I tried to be funny and asked with a knowing smile, "What's your name?"

He stared at me for at least five seconds before answering. "It's Steve. What's your name?"

"Sandra" was all that tripped out of my mouth. Not funny at all, but I couldn't think of anything else to say.

Orlando replied, "Nice to meet you," and then we parted ways.

At one point during the night when I came out of the washroom, Orlando was standing there with some people. "Hi 'Steve,'" I said.

His acquaintances replied instead. "That's his cover name."

We talked for a while and he told me he was working in Toronto the next day. I then asked, "What time do you have to be up in the morning?" I wanted to make conversation, but it sounded a bit sexual so I back-pedaled just a little bit. We continued talking until Orlando said, "Anyway, it was nice to meet you" and left.

Then, when I met up with Tatiana and we exchanged stories, she told me about something strange that had happened to her at the Century Room. Some guy was talking to her about a chinchilla fur. He went on and on about it and wouldn't leave her alone. Then a big African American guy looked at her and nudged his head as if to say, *Do you want me to take him out of here?* She nodded once and then he grabbed the chinchilla dude with both hands and whisked him away. He never bothered her again after that.

At 2:00 a.m. Tatiana and I took a cab back to my condo. When we arrived back at my condo I frantically paged through my journal so I could show her what I had written about my

Orlando Bloom dream. The journal entry said that I met him in a bar. As soon as she read that, she called her husband in Winnipeg, even though it was 3:00 a.m. his time. She told him about my dream, what I had journaled, and what had happened that night. That experience shows dreams sometimes do come true, even if they are wild dreams.

CHAPTER 11

Insensitive Healthcare

It had been a little more than ten years since my second hospitalization in 1997. I hadn't been on any psychiatric medications since January of 1998, and I was doing and feeling well. There was no stress, no medication, no side effects, and no thinking about having bipolar.

However, in January 2008, when I tried to get a family physician in Toronto, bipolar crossed my mind because of something on the intake form. When I discussed it with the female physician she was snotty and rude. She made me feel awful and said she would not take me on as a patient unless she had all my medical records from the time I was ill. I knew there were at least four chart books full from my hospital time, but come on—that was at least ten years ago. There were tears in my eyes as I walked down the stairs, out of her office, and onto King Street. I couldn't understand how a healthcare practitioner could be so insensitive.

When I told Karen my story, she listened intently and then gave me the name of her family physician. The doctor she recommended was wonderful, caring, compassionate, and considerate—everything I wanted in a family doctor. Also, because I hadn't had any sign of mental illness for at least five years, the new physician didn't require my history. Her kindness quickly made me forget about the snotty, rude physician.

Ryan

One Saturday night in January 2008, out on the patio at Brant House, a man approached me while Lindsay was off somewhere having a cigarette. Ryan was angelic looking, about six foot two, dressed preppyish, had blue eyes, and was extremely sweet to talk to. We were engaged in a relaxed conversation by the time Lindsay got back. She was upset he was talking to me and not her. She didn't like the idea of men being attracted to me instead of her, but Ryan told me outright that he wasn't interested in Lindsay.

Ryan and I exchanged numbers and went out a few times. When we stayed home, he cooked for me, which was very sweet, and we watched television; we both particularly liked *Seinfeld*. One night he asked if I wanted to watch the film *Bee Movie*. I hadn't seen a cartoon in years, but I really enjoyed it, not only because Jerry Seinfeld voiced the main character, but also because I really liked being in Ryan's company.

There was, however, one issue with him that was a turn-off for me—he smoked weed every day and I wasn't interested in doing that. It definitely threw a wrench in things, but we still continued to stay friends.

Soccer

A few days later while walking at dusk along Bathurst Street, a guy with short reddish-brown hair got off the streetcar. He seemed to come out of nowhere, and when he thought he had scared me, he quickly apologized. When I found out he lived in the same high-rise building as me, I struck up a conversation. He said he was on his way home after playing soccer, and asked if I was interested in playing. His team was looking for substitute players. We exchanged numbers, and I ended up playing with his team at their next indoor game.

Shortly after that at a condo party downtown, Karen introduced me to her Portuguese friend from work. Ken and I started talking about soccer and I agreed to play with his mixed male/female team—the second soccer team in Toronto I was playing for.

When two girls approached me from the first team and asked if I would also play on their all-girls team, I thought, *Why not.* That was an interesting team because it was a lesbian team. Initially I wondered, *Do they think I'm a lesbian? Do they like me that way?* But I quickly put those thoughts out of my mind. My goal was to play soccer and that was all that mattered.

And that's how I went from no soccer to playing three times a week, at three different fields, with three different teams.

Valentine's Disaster

When Ryan asked me out for Valentine's Day, I reluctantly declined because I had already promised Karen and Lindsay I would go out with them. But all the while the three of us were out that night, I secretly wished I was with Ryan.

At one point when we were out on the patio at Brant House, Lindsay disappeared to socialize. I didn't see it happen, but at some point she fell on her wrist and smacked her head against a metal claw-like handle sticking out of the wall. The bar immediately called us a cab to go to the hospital, and said that because it would take too long to get our coats from the coat check, they would hold onto them for us.

Both Lindsay and Karen had been drinking, and by the time we got to emergency, Lindsay was belligerent. My brother Michael is an emergency room doctor, which is how I knew the E.R. staff sometimes sobered people up before seeing them. In her drunken state, Lindsay was being particularly rude to the doctor, so they let her sit there to get some of the alcohol out of her system. I eventually went home a little after 4:00 a.m., but Lindsay and Karen were there until sometime after 5:00 a.m. Valentine's Day was ruined; I should have accepted Ryan's invitation instead.

Another Audition

Soon after that disastrous event, Ryan and I went out for Thai food. Back at my place, I noticed a voicemail on my cell phone. When I listened to it, I was so excited but I didn't say anything. The guy doing the superhero movie wanted me to audition for a commercial. I was so excited, all I could think about was getting Ryan to leave quickly so I could start preparing for my audition. And that's when I decided acting was the only boyfriend I really wanted. In the end, however, the real reason Ryan and I burned out was because of the weed.

Acting

At the end of soccer season, I started acting classes. I took acting on-camera, scene study, and commercial workshops—pretty much anything I could. The video camera made me nervous at first, but the feeling of acting and being in the moment was amazing. There was nothing I loved to do more. I spent hours in my condo practising my scenes, and I learned quickly which coloured clothing looked good on camera. The classes uplifted me and were a break from the chaotic business of cookie sales.

Stage Combat

Stage combat is a technique used in theatre that creates the illusion of physical combat without hurting the performers. The goal is to make the audience believe the fight is real. An acting teacher once told me, "Every actor should have stage combat on their resume because it will increase their chances of working in the film industry."

Because I was extremely interested in stunt work, I took a two week vacation from work and signed up for a stage combat course. The course ran for two weeks, from May 4 to 17, with only two days off. By the end of each day I was exhausted, but I loved every minute of it. There were essentially three parts to the course—single sword, quarterstaff, and unarmed—and we also learned fun stunts like how to fall off a table. One day we played a game with plastic knives, and although I forget the specific concept, I remember the game was about agility and quickness. One of the instructors told me I was freakishly fast.

At the end of the course, each participant performed the three parts of the course with dialogue. Afterward, three of the instructors/fight directors took each person into the weapon/equipment room and told us how we did. They told me I had failed the sword portion of the course. One of the fight directors seemed to be a little upset when he saw tears swelling in my eyes. As I looked up to that director I took his words to heart when he added, "Do not give up on the sword because it is an art form. It took me seven years to get it right." I just hoped life had a road mapped out for me that included acting and stunt work.

All Out of Whack

My body was all out of whack from my fitness competitions, and I hadn't had my period since I last competed in June 2007. By the following April when I still hadn't had my period, I talked to my doctor about it. She confirmed that was sometimes the result of intense training. I decided to try acupuncture.

On my way out of the treatment room after the fourth session of acupuncture and cupping, I felt very dizzy. The acupuncture hurt that day, which was unusual, so I went into the drugstore and walked around for a bit. Then I had a craving for a coffee, so I picked up a cup at Tim Horton's, but I only managed a couple of sips, which was very strange given how much I love coffee. Then, as I was walking through Fort York, my brain all of a sudden connected. It no longer felt like it was in two parts. *How odd.* By the time I got back to my suite, I went to the washroom and discovered I had my period. *AHHHHH*. I never thought I would say that about my period, but it was a feeling of relief.

In my condo I never stopped eating. I'd eat and eat and eat and never get full. It was directly related to the fitness competitions the previous year. The diets my trainers had me on meant that I had to force feed myself to eat the proper amount of protein so I would gain muscle. When I trained there was so much beef in the diet it was like eating half a cow. For a whole year after the competitions I struggled to know when I was hungry and when I was full. It was a constant battle for me because the whole training process made food a weapon. As a result of my eating post-competition, I gained weight and my self-esteem plummeted.

Paul

Tatiana came to visit me again in June after she had competed in and won another bodybuilding competition. On the Saturday we went shopping to outlet stores on Orfus Road and then ventured out to a bar on Wellington Street. The bar had small pristine pools outside on the patio, and the setting was serene. Lindsay and Karen again declined our invitation to hang out. Tatiana borrowed my Guess leopard dress that I used to wear in my early twenties. Her body was so fit and she looked great in it.

While we were there a guy with blonde hair walked down the stairs to the patio. He immediately caught my attention. Tatiana and I somehow ended up talking to him and his friends beside one of the pools. Paul was a teacher, stood five foot nine, had high cheek bones, messy short blonde hair, and dark eyes, and he dressed well. He also had a very lovely European accent. I mostly talked to Paul while Tatiana talked to his friends.

After Tatiana left for Winnipeg, Paul and I started hanging out together. We got on well enough, but most of the time that we dated he felt more like a friend to me. Still, we joked and laughed together and even pulled pranks on the people who worked in the building where I lived; they also did things back to us. One time they knocked on my door and when I answered there was nobody there but a big stuffed dog. Paul and I laughed and laughed. We definitely had fun together.

One night Paul and I were out for dinner. At the restaurant before the meal arrived, I was putting on Mac lip gloss when he said, "It is rude for you to put on lip gloss in the restaurant." *Well, it's rude for you to say so.* Although I couldn't exactly pinpoint why, that's when I suspected he was not the guy for me. Something about our relationship just felt wrong.

The best thing Paul did for me was stop me from eating to "completion"—what he called not eating until you are completely full. He helped me learn to listen to my stomach so I would not eat myself to death. And for that, I am very grateful for his time in my life.

CHAPTER 12

My Passion and Aspirations

My wildest dreams were to be an actress and do stunts. When I was hospitalized in my teens, my passion for acting really took hold, and it never went away, even though I didn't study it until I got to Toronto. The only people who knew about my love of acting were my parents. I never told any of my friends because I was afraid they would judge me and say, "An actress needs a real job to survive." When they asked what I was doing on evenings when I had an acting class, I would simply say, "Taking a class." I quietly continued my pursuit of acting and stunts, and decided not to tell people about my dreams until one of my auditions resulted in me being cast in something that would definitely come to fruition.

Often in Toronto I wondered why some of the people I met did not aspire to do things, to think outside the box, to challenge themselves. They didn't set goals or try to achieve them. They just settled into their lives, their jobs, their homes, and lived. I did everything I could to consistently push boundaries, set goals, and pursue my passions, and my passion was acting.

Even without an agent I still got auditions, including in New York and Los Angeles. One time I had one in New York on the way to a stunt audition for Universal Studios in L.A. That was tricky timing. There was another audition in Toronto for a role that paid well, but you had to be nude in the audition and my heart couldn't do it.

During my last acting class in Toronto a bunch of the students were walking out together. Suddenly, one of the students, a handsome guy about seven years younger than me, told me, "You're enigmatic." That flattered me because there were girls trying to hit on him, yet he was more interested in my mysteriousness. That wasn't the first time I had heard that in my life.

I loved being in Toronto, but every project and every class I studied told my soul that in order to fully live my dreams and pursue my passion, I needed to be in L.A. My heart had a hunger and a desire to be in that city, and the energy always felt right whenever I was there. So I made the decision to leave my job, my condo, and my life, and put all my things in storage. My parents came to Toronto to help me pack a couple of weeks before I left.

At the same time I was trying to get everything done, I was re-taking the sword class I had failed. Learning the choreography and the dialogue for the scene was difficult and challenging, but I was happy when I finished the class and passed it. Packing up my whole life and fitting what I needed into one hefty green and black Adidas backpack and one large suitcase to begin my journey to L.A. was a stressful experience.

There were many parts of my life that I left in Toronto. When Karen and I went out for dinner with some friends before I left, Lindsay didn't come, and that hurt my feelings. She just sent a card and didn't come out to say goodbye. Paul was another part I left in Toronto. I was more interested in him as a friend, even though he was more interested in something romantic. The last night before I left Toronto he came to dinner with us at my aunt and uncle's in Oakville, and when I said goodbye to him, tears streamed down his face. My eyes welled up, too, but I didn't cry. I had become very good at pushing down my emotions and not expressing what I really felt. Although I was sad to leave him, I knew he was not the one. I also knew there was something in L.A. I needed to achieve, and that I would do what was necessary to make that happen.

Then, right before I left, one of my best friends phoned me from Winnipeg. Emma was getting married, and asked me to be in her wedding party. "It will be in Winnipeg on Valentine's Day next year."

"Yes," I told her. "I will be in your wedding."

Remembrance Day

Uncle Gerald drove me to Toronto Pearson International Airport on November 11, 2008, to catch my flight to California. In the trunk of his car was my backpack and suitcase, as well as a nifty little fold-up bicycle that was so compact I could easily check it. I was going to use that bicycle to get to acting classes. My uncle hugged me and wished me good luck when he dropped me off outside the terminal.

The one-day journey would take me from the east coast to the west coast—from Toronto to Newark (New Jersey) to Phoenix (Arizona) and finally to Burbank (California). It was the second time in four months I had done the trip to

L.A.—the first time was to audition for stunts for a job that would have taken me to Universal Studios in Osaka, Japan.

Inside the airport they completely raked me over the coals. After checking my suitcase and loading my carry-on items onto the security scanner, I went through customs where an Asian lady patted me down. As she was frisking me, she said, "Think of it as a free Asian massage." That made me feel uncomfortable even though I knew it was a joke.

Then for some reason, security approached me and told me my situation was an "emergency." Apparently after my backpack was scanned, they used a security wand that recorded something suspicious.

I was taken aside and interrogated by one of the security managers. He said the substance they found was TPC-1 and that it was probably because I was carrying a lot of cosmetics. I didn't understand what the heck he was talking about, and I certainly didn't appreciate his insinuation.

At one point, the manager bowed his head, his arms in a prayer-like position. There was a moment of silence, during which I also bowed my eyes.

After he was finished he looked up and glared at me. "Do you know it's Remembrance Day?"

I smiled. "Yeah, I know." And then in a calm voice, I said, "There is only one soldier left who fought in the First World War and he is one hundred and eight years old. He lives in Seattle, Washington."

"How do you know that?" My interrogator seemed rather surprised, almost as if he had already decided I wasn't intelligent.

I was tempted to say, "On the radio," because that would have shown my innate ability to pay attention to detail.

Instead I answered, "My uncle told me." I decided instead to show him I had family who supported me.

A few minutes later, the manager took me back to where my carry-on luggage was waiting. He didn't say anything else, so I assumed they had searched and not found anything.

An apology would be nice.

I thought I was done, but in Newark Airport I had to somehow pack my purse into my already-full backpack because U.S. regulations only allowed one piece of carry-on luggage, either a purse or a backpack, but not both. When the attendant took my ticket he suggested I relax. My arms were shaking from the repack and the weight of my now fifty-five-pound backpack, which included my purse, heavy laptop, and bulky shoes, among other things.

By the time I finally boarded the plane, I was frustrated and exhausted from the not-so-fun experience that happened to me at Pearson International Airport.

The Final Leg

Fortunately, most of my trip passed without incident, at least until the final leg. When I boarded my flight to Burbank, I found a lady sitting in my window seat. I checked my ticket, then looked at the seat number, then looked at her and smiled. "You're in my seat."

Instead of responding at all, the woman started talking in Spanish to the person sitting in the aisle seat. When she asked that person a question, Spanish words flew out of my mouth in order to get her attention. "*Yo tengo doce,*" I said. *I have twelve.* Then I continued speaking in Spanish as I asked to see her ticket.

There was a cute blonde-haired, blue-eyed guy sitting behind us, watching the scene intently. He looked like a young Neil Patrick Harris, but better looking. I apologized to him because I knew the whole scene was a little distracting.

He replied, "Oh no, you're doing better than I could."

There was also an African American guy sitting two rows behind where I was supposed to be sitting. He looked at me with some amazement as I spoke to the woman in Spanish. He probably wouldn't have been surprised at all if he knew I had lived in Mexico for a while.

Eventually, the Spanish woman's *hija matrimonio* (daughter through marriage) helped straighten out where she was supposed to sit, which was beside me in the aisle seat. There were only two seats on either side of the aisle.

As long as I have my window seat, that's all I need.

The woman and I ended up talking for a while, during which time the only other issue we had was when she reached over to shut off my air. She said she was cold, and even though she must have seen the sweat dripping from my face, that air vent stayed shut.

The Spanish woman had the most gorgeous light auburn eyes, and her dark brown greyish hair was tied back to reveal her oval face. She had many wrinkles, each of which I knew told a story. She was dressed in a black skirt, stockings, and a heavy sweater, and wore a cheap gold watch. I imagined her to be very beautiful when she was younger.

Through our brief conversation, I learned she was from Guadalajara, Mexico, and had relatives in Burbank and Washington. She seemed uneasy when I asked her about the

U.S., and I wondered if she was there legally. Shortly after that, she moved forward to sit with her daughter. *Why didn't she sit there when she first boarded the plane?*

It wasn't until about twenty minutes later that my brain made the connection of what *matrimonio* meant. The delay in processing that information was because my mind tries to forget that "marriage" word.

My flight into Bob Hope International Airport was smooth and otherwise uneventful, but the rest of that night was a bit of a mixed bag. Unfortunately, because we landed late at night, and because the hostel where I was staying while in L.A. wouldn't take people in after 6:00 p.m. at night, I was booked into a cheap room for that night only in a hotel in Burbank. Fortunately, I only had to wait for about fifteen minutes before their shuttle picked me up from the airport. Unfortunately, my backpack and my bicycle were already heavy on my shoulders and I also had to carry my suitcase, so it didn't help when I found out there wasn't an elevator and I had to lug everything up the stairs to my room.

Welcome to California.

CHAPTER 13

Wednesday November 12, 2008

I woke up at 5:00 a.m. L.A. time—8:00 a.m. in Toronto. It always takes a while for my internal clock to adjust to any time change. After getting dressed, I went down for breakfast in the open air restaurant of the hotel lobby. When my order arrived, I quietly said, "Holy dyna!" to the server. I had forgotten how massive the portion sizes were in the U.S.

Almost immediately, I sent my too-runny eggs back to the kitchen to be cooked some more, but in hindsight, I should have left them there because I actually struggled to eat even *half* my breakfast. Fortunately, my brain reminded me to stop eating before my stomach was full. It was a great feeling for my body to be in tune with itself.

As I sat back with a cup of strong coffee, I soaked up the scenery of palm trees and relaxed in the reflection of the hotel's immaculate pool. I smiled the whole time because I knew I was exactly where I needed to be.

After breakfast, I checked out of the hotel and boarded the shuttle for the hostel in North Hollywood. It had been recommended to me by an individual at the first acting school I was going to attend in North Hollywood; most of the people who stayed at the hostel were in their twenties and studying acting or music. When we arrived, the shuttle driver and I were greeted by a surfer dude about six foot with chin length, dirty blonde hair, and big blue eyes. His parents owned the hostel and he ran it for them. At first he was really nice and friendly, but the next time I stayed there, he turned cold on me.

In many ways it felt more like a house than a hostel. When I first walked in, there was a long hall that separated two areas. Each had a kitchen with a granite countertop, and a common area with couches and a sixty-plus-inch television; the laundry was shared by everyone. There were bedrooms on the first and second floor, and although there were some private rooms, they were double the money. I didn't mind sharing with two others because we were all there to pursue acting or some other form of creative expression.

I didn't meet them right away, but initially I had two roommates. One was leaving for New Mexico two days after I arrived, so I didn't really get to know her, but the other was Wendy. She wasn't around on weekends because she did the lighting and sound for her friend's band, was a music student, and also worked for an independent label. She was short, and had glasses and a facial piercing. She was bangerish.

After I put my things in my room, the dude drove me to the grocery store to get some food. As we talked, I realized he was a little high maintenance—too particular about the material things he just *had* to have. My parents always taught me "Material things can be replaced; people can't."

As we were driving back from the grocery store, I "met" Fabio. He was five foot eleven and had a chiselled jaw line, messy blonde curly hair, and a goatee. He was lean, and had blue eyes and perfect teeth. As Fabio was crossing the intersection, the dude honked at him and offered him a ride. Fabio looked at us, flipped us the bird, and then pulled his pants down and mooned us in mid-afternoon. I so wished I had my camera.

Back at the hostel, Fabio insisted on telling me his story. At first I was happy to listen, but it was complicated and messy and apparently never ending. He shared the same birthday as Paris Hilton—February 18, which is right in between Pisces and Aquarius—and he spoke Greek and Italian. In fact, he said he was some big star in Italy because he had won a reality show, and that is where he met his girlfriend Melana. They were together for two years, half of which he was depressed and all of which took away *his* energy. He said she was a Pisces like me, and that we had a lot of similar qualities. I wasn't sure that was such a good thing. When I asked where Melana was, he said she was filming in Mexico, had recently got a boob job, worked as a model and a TV host, and was about to release an album. He thought that he was more famous than her and that she was jealous of him.

Their relationship somehow included her ex-boyfriend who was the cameraman for the TV show she hosted. Fabio believed Melana got her ex that job just to make Fabio jealous. After Melana reinforced that possibility by telling the tabloids Fabio wouldn't be with her twenty-four hours a day, he had a phone interview with the Italian press about his situation. I told him she was probably just looking for media attention, and suggested, "Don't give away all the milk for free, especially if you expect them to buy the cow." In other words, don't spill your guts to the media if you want them to come back to you later on.

By the time Fabio started explaining how he had logged onto Melana's Facebook account pretending to be her so he could send a message to her ex-boyfriend and how that was the start of their breakup, it all became a little too much. In hindsight, I took in a lot of information in only a day, and there wasn't any time to really process it. The whole conversation drained my energy, which is often a side effect of always trying to help others.

Throughout my life, people have trusted me because of how well I listen, and also because I don't judge them. I can easily pick up on other people's energies and feelings, and I always want to help them. What I should be doing instead is helping myself by focusing on me and taking care of myself.

Change for the Worse

On Thursday night, after listening to Fabio for most of the day, I cycled to my comedy class at an acting school in Burbank. On Friday November 14, I recopied my notes from the comedy class and I rang Michael Longley, who did stunt work for the *Transformers* film. Erica who worked with me in cookie sales had given me his contact information. They had gone to high school together, and she had emailed him on my behalf. Toward the end of our conversation, Michael invited me to the *Transformers* wrap party on the Saturday night. A wrap party is a celebration for the cast and crew of the film when filming of a movie is finished. It was my first one, and I was so looking forward to it.

The next day, the air outside the balcony at the hostel smelled fresh and combined nicely with the scent of the laundry softener being used down the hall. I was at peace with myself and wrote in my journal:

"I will always suggest for people to go outside the box that they live in. I have always learned so much about myself this way. I am doing what I am supposed to do. I am excited to be here and there is sunshine. I am tranquil and where I need to be. Life is good."

I had lived the previous ten years or so without any symptoms of bipolar. I had been free of the stigma, free of any medication, and free from an illness that had haunted my entire existence. My mind had found a way to elude that illness. I didn't think about it, didn't question it, and didn't worry about it. I just lived.

But by Sunday November 16, 2008, my life had changed for the worse.

Weekend Hell

Different people come into your life at different times. Three days after I arrived at the hostel, my friend Sheila came to visit me, and we were out for the entire weekend.

When we both lived in Winnipeg, we hung around in the same crowds, but eventually she moved to California. I made a point to visit her there almost every year for the next seven years. We shopped, laughed, danced at bars, ate food from ethnic restaurants, and often ate late-night breakfasts out. It was good old-fashioned girly fun right when you needed it.

Part of me always tries to look out for other people, which is why that friendship with Sheila harpooned my heart. Even though we shared good times together, I felt sorry for her—she could be very difficult—and did whatever I could to be a friend. However, she often pissed me off when she got moody and adopted the attitude of it's her way or no way. I remember sitting in the passenger seat of her car once as she talked and talked about something she was blatantly wrong about. When I tried to say what I thought, she wouldn't listen; she only believed that she was right. My response was to stay quiet and look out the passenger window. She could argue for hours, even if she was wrong. So, yes, we often had fun, but it ticked me off when she was moody and always had to be right.

Looking back now, for my own well-being, I should never have left the hostel that weekend.

The first night out Sheila and I went to a club and danced, after which we went to Swingers to eat. Among other things, Swingers served interesting organic egg breakfasts, and the décor reminded me of a fifties diner. It had a great orange island space with swivel chairs. The after-club crowd was in their twenties and thirties. Take me out for a really good breakfast and I am sold. They are my favourite meals to go out for, possibly because of my coffee addiction.

There were three guys at the diner who asked if they could join us at our booth. Mark had short spiky blonde hair and light eyes, and we instantly got along. Part of the reason I liked him was because he was a fan of the Edmonton Oilers. My brother Michael raised me to love the Oilers, and in my experience, it was difficult to find an American who loved hockey, especially a Canadian team.

Eddy was an actor. He was extremely pretty with his chiselled jawline, dark hair, and dark eyes. He was into Sheila and he told her, but she wasn't interested because she only dated a certain race, and he was not the race she dated.

T.J. was African American with a shaved head and brown eyes. He was very talkative and kept the conversation going by asking all the questions. He was so into Eddy that you would almost think he had a crush on him. T.J. built Eddy up and inflated his ego, but Eddy didn't need that because he already had enough of an ego. Before we went back to our room at the Beverly Laurel Motor Hotel, Mike gave me his number and T.J. gave Sheila his.

Saturday morning I was excited and talked to Sheila about the *Transformers* wrap party. She was cold about it and said she didn't want to spend any money on a dress. That both disappointed and annoyed me, but I should have expected it. Sheila made a good salary, but she never seemed to have any money, which was always hard for me to grasp.

CHAPTER 14

Going Astray

Saturday afternoon while Sheila napped, my mind began going astray.

The hotel had a courtyard with trees, a pool, and lounge chairs. I took my MP3 player down to the pool. It still had the same songs on it from the first time I downloaded my music. All of a sudden tears began streaming down my face. They were uncontrollable. So nobody could see my tears, I lay on my stomach on the white lounger chair with my headphones in. Slow songs played over and over again on my MP3 player, including "You're Beautiful" by James Blunt. My body began convulsing, and there was a pain in my heart that would not go away.

My brother Michael was on my mind, but I don't remember anything else I was thinking. I sobbed so hard that it hurt every point of my existence. My eyes watered until my tear ducts ran out of tears. After two hours of my sides in pain and with no tears left, I called Michael and we had a normal conversation. He always made me feel better, no matter what the situation. Eventually I went back up to the room. Sheila didn't have the slightest idea that I had bawled my eyes out at the pool.

I can't blame people for not knowing. Because of the anosognosia, when my mind goes astray I don't even believe I have bipolar, which is why I can't talk to anyone about what is going on inside me. I can't tell them what is wrong with me, and I especially can't tell them about what I am thinking because I think all my delusions are huge secrets.

Before psychosis takes over my mind, there are signs that something might be amiss. One of those signs is tears, lots and lots of unexplained and uncontrollable tears, sometimes a day or two beforehand. I am aware of those signs, but once my mind goes manic, my brain tells me instead that everything is marvellous and wonderful and headed in the right direction. It is the scariest place to be. Even now, my heart pains and makes my body weak when I think about it. About bipolar me. Bipolar me is the haunting of the brain where it thinks it is smarter than everyone.

A Big Mistake

After Sheila woke up from her nap, I convinced her to go with me to the Beverly Center to shop for dresses, among other things. In one particular store, three associates helped me. The first one brought a couple of different dresses, the second shoes, and the third a belt. Meanwhile, Sheila ho-hummed about buying a thirty-dollar dress. She said she didn't want to put out the money if there was even the slightest chance we weren't getting into the wrap party. That made me feel bad for her and I bought a bracelet for her to wear that night.

After the mall we went back to the hotel to get ready. Sheila wore wedge sandals and the mauve fitted dress that she'd ho-hummed about buying. My outfit consisted of a black silk-like flowy dress and a thick synch belt with a blingy circle. My shoes were black with a six-inch heel that was chunky at the top and narrow at the bottom. My long blonde hair was curled with hot rollers and bounced off my shoulders. My make-up was simple and innocent. My favourite part of my outfit was the long dark green jacket that fit my body. The jacket was in between a plastic and a suede material and it brought everything together. Green matches my eyes and is a favourite colour of mine.

When we were ready, we drove from the hotel to the party. Just as we were pulling into a parking spot, Michael rang to say he couldn't make it to the party because of the wildfires in California, but reassured me we should still be able to get in.

The woman at the door wore thick framed glasses and held a clipboard. When she asked the name, I said, "Michael Longley."

She asked, "Is he coming?"

My eyebrows went upward as I explained, "He can't make it because of the wildfires."

She looked at me questionably. "How do you know him?"

My answer was a big mistake. "He's a friend of a friend."

"A friend of a friend?" Her nose went up in the air. "I'm sorry I can't let you in."

Sheila immediately sighed and started walking away. She wouldn't talk to me because she was pissed off. The whole night was ruined.

The Cold Shoulder

As we walked toward Sheila's car in silence, her phone rang. It was T.J. She didn't want to talk to him because she was upset. And that was what she did when she was upset—she either snapped at you or ignored you. Sometimes she would snap at you *and* ignore you. She handed me the phone and climbed into her car. T.J. asked if we wanted to meet them at Big Wangs.

Sheila said no.

Screw it. She is not wasting my night.

When I told her I was going to meet the guys, she simply drove off. Fortunately, the lounge was close to the wrap party, and even with my six inch heels, I managed to walk to Big Wangs without any problem. Inside was Eddy with a girl and T.J. with a rose. T.J. handed me the long-stemmed red rose. Tears were streaming down my face. They were uncontrollable. He told me not to cry and said everything would be okay. I snapped the rose.

"Why did you do that?"

I didn't say anything.

The way Sheila treated me had really upset me. She didn't get the outcome she hoped for with the wrap party, so she turned cold on me. She walked away from the lady with the clipboard, then walked away from me and ignored me. She tried to make me feel guilty, and her bad-tempered attitude wounded my heart. I couldn't tell T.J. any of that, the only thing I could do was take my emotions out on the rose.

At Big Wangs we sat at a high top table. There were many sports games and highlights playing on the multiple television screens. The vibe was sporty, hip, and cool. T.J. commented how nice I looked; he said I looked like a superhero with my long green jacket. Eddy's girlfriend, as it turned out, looked at me and simply said, "I never dress up." She was beautiful, petite with long golden blonde hair and light blue eyes, but was wearing denim and flip flops. That really pissed me off. My teeth bit my bottom lip to prevent me from saying anything.

What I really wanted to tell her was, "Maybe you *should* dress up, and then your boyfriend wouldn't try to pick up other women like my friend Sheila." But instead of saying that I gave her a half smile. The restroom was calling my name so I excused myself from the table and shed more tears in the privacy of a cubicle. When I returned, we sat and talked for a while. T.J. tried to hit on me most of the night, but I rejected him. He wasn't my type.

After Big Wangs we dropped Eddy's girlfriend off at her house. She hugged and kissed him and told him she loved him before he drove off to hit on other chicks. Then we stopped at 7 Eleven. I didn't have any idea who Eddy was, but I decided he must have been really famous because from the back seat of the car I could see a lot of camera flashes going off. Girls were trying to hug him and put their arms around him and all sorts of things.

After 7 Eleven we went to Swingers. T.J. called Sheila and somehow convinced her to meet us there. It was around 1:00 a.m. and we were sitting in a booth with orange seats when she arrived. Sheila was quiet at first and gave me the cold shoulder, which was normal after a disagreement. I knew what she was like and I knew how to act around her. Maybe that was why I wanted to be an actress—because I acted with her all the time. I knew there were only certain ways you could step with her before you got your hand slapped.

A few times during the night, Eddy looked me in the eyes and stung me with his words. "I don't want you, I want your friend."

My mind couldn't understand that comment. *I haven't given you any indication I am even interested.*

He also made a lot of facial expressions, moving his eyebrows up and down and doing silly things with his lips.

"Aren't actors supposed to talk with their eyes?" I asked as I raised my own eyebrows.

When he said he had heard that a lot before, I wondered if he really was a good actor, or if he had only made it because of his looks.

After a few hours, Eddy was hitting on a waitress outside Swingers and T.J. was talking to another group of people. With only ourselves for company and conversation, Sheila and I decided we'd had enough. We made our way back to our hotel and went to sleep.

Click!

When the bipolar mind has an episode or the individual becomes manic, there can be periods of excitement where you feel over-stimulated like you can fly or you have delusions or hallucinations or both. A world is created where you think you are on the most perfect path, but in fact the path you are on is muddy, claylike, it's pouring rain, and you don't have rubber boots. You're soaking wet. Pretty shitty.

When my mind goes astray, I have mastered hiding that I am ill. I never vocalize what my mind is thinking. My mom is usually the first to recognize my illness, but sometimes, because I hide it so well, not even she can tell my mind has gone astray.

When I'm in this state I have frank psychotic episodes. These are episodes that are readily apparent because they are heralded by manic symptoms—characterized by elevated and expansive moods and followed by delusional thought patterns. A lot of bipolar individuals have up and down mood symptoms, but that is not what happens for me. Instead, during my episodes I have hours of tears for one or two days in the first five days of onset, but after that I am only manic. I have never become depressed after a manic episode.

When you are bipolar, it's like the chain on a light is pulled—Click!—and suddenly you "switch" into a different world. The only thing that can pull me back from that world is medication, but finding the right combination of meds to do that is a constant struggle. Eventually, the medication does start to work, the chain is pulled again, and the light goes out on that world. It is completely gone and I start to be well again.

If I had to pinpoint my bipolar that time in L.A., I would definitely say my mind clicked over sometime on Sunday November 16.

Time to Check Out

That morning we checked out of the Beverly Laurel. To thank Sheila for visiting, I paid for the hotel, even though things hadn't quite gone as I had planned. I often brought her gifts or groceries or meals because she would let me stay at her place. She often told me how much she appreciated me visiting her and that she enjoyed my company. I like Sheila, but I just wish she could have found a way to keep her moods to herself and not let them intrude on and hurt our friendship.

After checking out we went back to Swingers for breakfast. I half expected to see T.J. still there, but those guys had all left. After I paid the bill—another thank-you—I folded the receipt up strategically into a tiny square.

When I looked up, Sheila was staring at me, like perhaps she thought I was acting a little funny. "What are you doing?"

My shoulders just shrugged.

After breakfast, we drove to Santa Monica and went shopping for the day. We found a herbal store that smelled of aromatherapy. Once inside, I saw greenery, herbs, teapots, and books. My brain told me I was a medicine woman and that I could heal other people. When my mind went through a manic episode, I could be anyone I wanted, even a medicine woman willing and able to help whoever I could. Ironic then that at the same time my mind was going through a mood disorder, I wanted to tell Sheila she needed help with *her* mood. I also wanted to tell her things I couldn't tell her when I was well.

In the herbal store we talked to a male member of the staff. My mind wanted to rescue Sheila by getting her on herbs that would cure her urinary tract infection. After talking to the store clerk, she ended up buying her own herbs, which was exactly what my bipolar mind wanted.

I bought an aromatherapy book, a small decorated Chinese teapot with a cup attached, a couple of stones (jade and rose quartz), some herbs, and a book about how to improve your mood. After leaving that store, we walked into T-Mobile on the corner of 4th and Wilshire. For some reason, almost immediately after we walked in, Sheila walked out again. I stayed because I needed to purchase a U.S. cell phone, and asked an associate to help me.

"I don't want my friend to see it," I said.

His voice went up a pitch as he said, "Really?" and then he gave me a plastic bag for it.

Quickly my hand grabbed the bag and tucked it into the other bag from the herbal store. I found Sheila waiting outside and we went into a jewellery store called Sea of Silver. I bought several beautiful pieces that added up to more than $500. With all of my other purchases, my $1000 limit on my credit card was maxed. I had already paid for the hotel, breakfast, my aromatherapy books, and a cell phone, but needed another $80 to pay for the jewellery. When I offered the guy my Victoria Secret gift card and told him there was $88 still on it, he was a bit surprised but took it anyway. Of course, it all made perfect sense to me. Then we spent some time in Victoria Secret before leaving Santa Monica at dusk.

Some of my purchases that day were made because I was manic. When you are bipolar and become manic you can go on a shopping spree where you buy things you do and don't need and spend lots of money you do or don't have. But it all makes sense at the time because when you are manic, everything becomes extreme. Shopping sprees like that are a clear sign that my mind is definitely going astray.

On the way back to L.A., we stopped at the home of one of Sheila's friends. At one point Sheila went to the restroom, and immediately after she came out, my brain told me that I had something that would start to erase her UTI. When I went into the restroom, my arm waved around the jade stone, cleaning the air around the toilet. Then I chucked the stone on the ground when I came outside.

A few minutes later Sheila picked the stone up off the white carpet, and asked, “What is this?”

My shoulders just shrugged.

We sat and talked and watched TV with Sheila’s friend. He was a really sweet guy and clearly liked her, but she wasn’t interested in him. Eventually we left and Sheila drove me back to the hostel where I was staying.

The way I remember that night, I arrived at the hostel, the iron-gate opened, and three different guys who stayed there helped carry my luggage and belongings from Sheila’s car. Then I was whisked inside the hostel. I never thought about saying goodbye to Sheila, but on the back seat of her car, I left the book about how to improve your mood.

When I talked to her on the phone a few months later, she commented, “You never came back to say goodbye.”

My mind was astray and it couldn’t go back, but I didn’t tell her that.

CHAPTER 15

A Closed Door

Monday morning, I walked to my acting class. It was close to the hostel and ran Monday through Friday full-time days. Then in the evenings twice a week I would bike to classes at an acting school in Burbank. The theatre for the full-time program was small, dark, and black, and the energy was all wrong. Before class started I sat in the waiting area filling out a form on a clipboard as tears streamed uncontrollably down my face. My brain didn't understand why I was crying. My arms quickly wiped away the tears so nobody would see them.

That first day didn't go well, partly because my manic mind believed people could change identities and be completely different people. It led me to think that was how people in Hollywood hid—by changing into another identity so nobody would recognize them. They had different facial features or a different colour or style of hair.

My ill mind thought the director of the school was my psychiatrist. Certain things like his hair colour and the way he dressed made me believe that.

Then, at the start of the class, all the students stood up and did a warm-up activity where you mirrored your partner's actions. When I mirrored my partner, I realized he had many features similar to my kickboxing instructor from Mexico. I never liked that instructor romantically, but my ill mind thought I was getting married and that my partner was one of my husbands. I don't know why marriage was part of my thinking because it had never been a priority in my life, but it was where my mind sometimes went when it was ill.

Without warning, tears began streaming down my face again, and when I kept wiping the tears away, I lost one of my contacts. My mind thought it was symbolic of me losing touch with that kickboxing "contact" in my life.

I rarely lost my contact lenses, but when I was ill I often threw them away. That was because I never wanted to relive the awful situations or circumstances that appeared in my mind while I was mentally ill. I thought if I put those contact lenses back in my eyes, my mind would think what I thought when I last wore them. So instead of re-living those nightmares, I tossed the contacts in the garbage. That ended up costing me a lot of money because I didn't wear disposable contacts.

Luckily I always carry a spare set of lenses in my bag, but after replacing the lost contact that day, I left the acting school without saying a word.

In my manic state my brain told me I couldn't go back to the way I lived before I was ill. The life ahead was far superior, a life where people lived forever. I called those people immortals. Their characteristics were like goddesses and gods. Immortals were able to do what they wanted, eat what they wanted without gaining weight, and change what they wanted, including their appearance and their lifestyle.

My brain told me that the identities of immortals overlapped. Facial features and hair changed when the individual took on a new identity. Their nose or the lines on their face or their hair or some other feature would change just enough to make them look different. My bipolar mind had delusions that one immortal could actually be five different people. I would see images in the media and look at a certain feature like their eyes, and say, "Darren is actually Karl and Karl is actually Mike and Mike is actually Christopher," when in fact they were all different people.

When all of those thoughts were brewing, I decided the right thing to do was go off my gluten-free diet. Before I moved to California, I was on that diet for several years. Back in 2004 while I was at university, my hand started cracking and bleeding. No topical medication the dermatologist prescribed for me would heal it. One of my textbooks had photos about celiac disease—where an individual cannot eat wheat, oats, barley or rye—and other skin conditions. When I saw the photos, I wondered if going off those foods would cure my hand. So I started eating gluten free and it worked. My hand no longer cracked and bled. When my dermatologist saw that my hand had cleared up, she said, "I love it when people solve their own problems."

My brain told me that since I was going to live forever anyway, I could eat whatever I wanted. And from then on I didn't go back to that diet.

The next day before class, I walked eight minutes to the café beside the acting school and bought a sandwich. I wanted to share it with the director of the acting school because my brain told me he was my psychiatrist, only in a different identity. My actual psychiatrist loved sandwiches and would often eat them during our sessions. I casually walked up the stairs to the second floor of the building where the director of the school's office was located. On the first day of classes, he told all the students, “My door is always open,” but when I knocked on the door, he wasn’t there. Although I couldn’t remember exactly what, my mind thought I had done something horribly wrong the day before, and I wanted to apologize to him. When he didn’t answer, I returned to the café, ate the sandwich at a table, wiped the crumbs from my face, and decided it was rebellion time.

Rebellious Me

I returned to the acting school, walked into the dark theatre, pushed down a black theatre seat, plopped myself down, and put in the white earplugs attached to my MP3 player. The words of the song I listened to made total sense to me because they were about my life. My brain told me those songs were a prediction made by people of what would happen to me. I thought everything to do with the media was directed at me. As I sat in that black theatre seat I enjoyed singing profanities out loud. I was rebelling. When I am well I don’t usually swear, and certainly don’t sing profanities out loud, but when my mind is ill, those things can certainly happen.

The director of the acting school yelled at me from across the room and tore a strip off me in front of everyone. I sat there, dumbfounded, but I simply took his lashes and didn’t talk back. Then he called me out of the class and kicked me out of the school. I stared at him and said, “You can’t kick me out. You have to show me where in the contract it says you can do that.” He did, and he also said he would refund my money.

When I asked for a recommendation for another school, he pointed to the Meisner school up the street.

That afternoon, I walked slowly up the street, past a shop with old, neat antique luggage in the window, until the Meisner school I was looking for came into view. Inside the theatre was dark and there were maroon-coloured theatre seats; on the stage were a dresser, a plant, and a few other props. I met with the acting teacher, who stood about five foot ten, had short curly brown hair but always wore a flat cap, and appeared to be in his thirties. Both he and his assistant interviewed me. Their questions were tough, but thanks to my taekwondo training, they bounced right off me. Taekwondo had taught me many things, including how to adapt and overcome situations, and also that if a door closes, as it had at the other school, I could kick another door open.

So I kicked that Meisner door open, figuratively speaking, of course. I had never taken a Meisner class before, but I learned that the focus there was on instinct and later emotions, the goal of which is to live truthfully under the given imaginary circumstances. That felt right for me, and I thought to myself, *Sometimes when something bad happens, something better comes along.*

After the interview, I walked back to the hostel, stopping at a place that sold huge lawn ornaments and fountains. My shoes shuffled around on the red clay ground. My mind, body, and soul had to refresh, rejuvenate, and move on from what happened at the first acting school. Waterfalls are serene and my happy place. My mind felt better and at ease beside the water fountains.

A Natural Cleanse

That night at the hostel, my mind and body were not at ease and I needed a cleanse. My brain told me that everything in my bedroom and the bathroom was not right and needed to be thrown in the garbage. I even threw out my roommate Wendy's toothbrush. That caused her to change rooms; she didn't want to stay with me anymore.

In my heart I felt bad about the toothbrush, so I went to a convenience store and purchased her a new one, bought a pack of condoms, and also shook cinnamon out of a spice bottle into a plastic cup from the coffee area. For a split second I thought I was manic, but that thought quickly left me.

Back at the hostel, I went into one of the kitchens and found coarse salt in the cupboard. With the cup of cinnamon in one hand and the coarse salt in the other, I went to the bathroom. My hand gently sprinkled the cinnamon on the ledge of the window in the shower because I had read in my aromatherapy book, "Those who have a cinnamon personality are described as strong personalities, affable, practical, intelligent and larger than life." (Battaglia, 2004)

I was definitely larger than life, or at least that was what my brain told me, and I still thought I was a medicine woman. I poured the coarse salt and water in the bottom of the bathtub, scrubbing my feet. My friend Sheila had a UTI and since I was a medicine woman and larger than life, I thought I needed to cleanse myself. My mind was upset. To alleviate my pain, I purchased the condoms as a joke—to offer protection to myself. A silly joke, perhaps, but my mind obviously needed some form of comedy to feel better. I also thought that I had possibly cured myself of my life-threatening seafood allergy.

Deadly Allergy

When I was eighteen months old, at some point after my mom sat me on the kitchen counter, I screamed at the top of my lungs. I had developed hives all over me and my bottom had swelled up. Clearly an allergic reaction, but to what, you ask? It was an allergy to fish. My mom being a nurse had talked to my pediatrician and knew to keep me away from it all of my life. I wasn't actually tested until I was fifteen. The allergy tests revealed I had a deadly allergy to fish. I was tested again for seafood when I was twenty-one, and the doctor said that even though I was only allergic to *some* seafood, he recommended staying away from it all, just in case the seafood touched each other in transportation. Plus, he said I could develop allergies to the seafood I wasn't allergic too.

The reason I thought I had cured myself of my allergy was because the previous night I had cooked up some maitake mushrooms in a frying pan with leftover Thai food. I had read somewhere that maitake mushrooms can help with immune regulation, inflammation, and allergies. My manic mind thought there was a possibility those mushrooms had cured my fish allergy, but in reality, that was not the case.

Later that afternoon my stomach had hunger pangs, so I wandered up the street to a Mexican restaurant. My brain told me I knew the people who worked in the restaurant, but they were just in different identities. I was wearing my scoop-necked purple shirt, black shorts and black ballet flats. My long blonde hair hung just below my shoulders, and I was wearing natural make-up with barely a hint of lip gloss. When I opened the door of the restaurant, my feet stepped inside and I sauntered over to the bar. I pulled back the wicker bar stool and sat close to a

Mexican with a long moustache, short dark hair, and brown eyes. He was drinking a Heineken, and I instantly thought he was my soon-to-be father-in-law in his Spanish identity.

When I placed my order, I told the server in Spanish that I was allergic to fish, even though my brain told me the medicine woman status plus the maitake mushroom meal the night before had cured my fish allergy.

The guy who worked behind the bar had a lazy eye. I thought he was my friend George in one of his identities because they looked similar with their blondish hair and light eyes. Also, George always told some silly joke about a lazy eye. My brain told me "George" would slip some fish into my food without my knowledge because he knew I was cured of my fish allergy. In any case, I was immortal and had the ability to live forever. Immortal people did not have allergies.

When my food arrived, there were tacos, quesadillas, refried beans, and white cheese on top. My fingers grabbed the quesadilla first. After a few bites I chewed and swallowed the food, and nothing happened. My hand then grabbed the large circular glass of *limonada* and washed the quesadilla down. Then I cut into the chicken tacos. My mind questioned whether it really was chicken or if the kitchen had actually fed me fish. Either way, I had no allergic reaction.

Occasionally, my bipolar brain would tell me something was safe or that I was cured of something, when in fact that was deadly wrong. So it made perfect sense to me that a kitchen would feed a customer fish even though they ordered chicken because they were allergic to fish. It made sense because I was in a manic state and my mind was off-balance.

As I sat on the wicker stool, I conversed with my soon-to-be father-in-law. All we talked about was the house he had built.

My brain told me that house was one of many built around the world for me and my soon-to-be husband.

Looking back, that entire conversation was weird, in more ways than one. Even when my mind was sound, I never wanted a husband. First and foremost, I wanted to act. That was my passion and I never let a guy stand in my way. To this day I still don't know where that husband bullshit came from.

The Bet

My soon-to-be Mexican father-in-law and I stood up and walked over to a tiled painting on the wall. It was approximately eight by five feet in dimension, with one-square-foot white glossy tiles. As we stood there and talked about the painting and the tiles, he asked, "Can I have a square?" Then he laughed out loud. In my ill, unbalanced mind, my brain had created a betting pool over a tiled painting of which that strange Mexican man wanted a square. The winner of the pool would receive the Heineken fortune because that was the beer the Mexican was drinking. So what was the bet about? It was about my wedding day, and which date I would tie the knot.

After I paid my bill, I left the restaurant. My feet in the black ballet flats sauntered along the sidewalk. I suddenly came to a payphone. My hand picked up the receiver. My parents had set up a 1-800 number that I or anyone in our family could use to call home when we were travelling or if we simply wanted to connect with each other. The rates were cheaper, so it was easy to call Winnipeg from anywhere in North America.

My finger dialed the number, and when I heard the tone, I punched in the access code and then the home number. Even when my mind was ill, my heart was still with my family. And my astray mind wanted my family to win the bet.

Mom answered the phone. "Hello?"

My voice trembled. "Hi, Mom. What date would you pick?"

She answered, "I don't know what you're talking about. You're not making sense."

I quickly responded, "I have to go. Bye." And then I hung up the phone.

I was frustrated. I knew if I wanted my family to win the bet I couldn't explain more to my mom for fear of disqualification from the pool. My brain told me I had to figure out the betting pool myself, so I walked back to the hostel where I was staying.

After talking to me, my parents knew something was very wrong. They tried to call the hostel several times, but the line was either busy or no one answered. Then they contacted Sheila, who tried to reach me but I refused to answer her call. Instead of driving to the hostel, which was only twenty minutes from her place, she asked her friend whose house we had been at to try and contact me *for* her. When I got his text, I did respond, although I still don't know why.

That night, I went to the Santa Monica Pier with T.J., the guy from Swingers and Big Wangs. I don't know why I went out with him; clearly, he was attracted to me, but I wasn't attracted to him. While we were at the pier, he kept making suggestive comments and put his arms around me, and afterward, we went back to the hostel where I sat on his lap in the common area—all things I would NEVER do. I am very protective of my own space, and don't like public displays of affection, even with a boyfriend. Why did my brain tell me to go out with him? Probably because when my mind is astray, I do things I would never normally do.

Fortunately, the next day my parents came to rescue me. They arrived at the hostel in the afternoon, packed up some of my belongings, and took me to a hotel—the same hotel where I started my journey in L.A. back on November 11. The first person I called after we got to the hotel was T.J. I was supposed to go out with him that night, but I told him I couldn't because my parents wanted me to go home. He tried unsuccessfully to talk me out of it.

Then I called my psychiatrist, who also said he wanted me to go back to Winnipeg. I often listen to my psychiatrist; he is irreplaceable. The amount of time and energy he has spent supporting me and my family is unbelievable and extremely rare. Any doctor who knows him will say how brilliant he is.

My parents and my psychiatrist convinced me to leave California. For some reason we left behind my expensive pair of boots bought at Winners, my fold-up bike, my long forest green vinyl superhero jacket, and some other belongings. When my parents arrived in Canada they returned my cell phone I bought at T-Mobile and cancelled the contract; they had a doctor's letter that proved I was ill.

My dreams had been interrupted. The pursuit of my passion had been put on hold. I cried my eyes out and sobbed for an entire leg of the flight home. The woman who sat next to me wished I would stop—I could see it in her face—but the tears continued to fall. There was no way to stop them.

Not only were my dreams shattered, but the illness I hated had resurfaced. All those years of not experiencing any symptoms of having bipolar and not needing medications had come back to haunt me. I swallowed the words bipolar with a lump in my throat, and every day my medications reminded me of my complexities. Learning to let go of bipolar and all of my complexities would become something my mind, heart, and soul would continually work on.

CHAPTER 16

Never a Bridesmaid

One of the first things I did when I got back to Winnipeg was call my best friend Emma. It was a cold December night when I took the silver portable phone from my parents' bedroom and went into the living room where I sat in an off-white chair with pastel floral patterns. The room was full of beautiful furniture pieces, including a black glossy Kawai piano that separated the kitchen from the living room, and the antique buffet Dad had sanded down and stained to give it a woody tone. I looked at the phone in my hand and dialed Emma's number.

Emma answered the phone. "Hello. How are you?"

"Okay. You?"

"Good."

"Um . . . I can't be in your wedding anymore." No other explanation. Only those words.

I knew she was upset, but I was relieved she didn't ask why not. There was no way I could tell her I was ill or that my parents came to rescue me from L.A. or that I had a mental illness, or anything else going on in my brain. There was no way I could tell her because my brain was telling me that I wasn't sick at all.

Before hitting the end button on the telephone, I simply said, "I can't talk about it right now. I have to go."

Instant relief.

My astray mind was working hard to hold things together. It told me I was a relationship expert and that her wedding shouldn't happen at all, but I couldn't tell Emma that. It pains me to this day to know that I hurt her. Emma had always been such a good friend, and we had gone through so much together—work, relationships, volunteering, travelling. But unfortunately, when my mind went astray, the only thing I could do was let the friendship go for a while.

The Kiss of Tea

In my parents' office I laid out blank pieces of papers in a square shape. I started to make art with the tea bag from my tea. I dabbed and blotted and made different designs on the paper, and I re-soaked the tea bag when necessary. Thoughts were racing around in my head about acting, the ups and downs of the stock market, the fashion world, and how they all connected to my tea bag art. So I sat down and wrote an idea for a television show about it all.

Fashion Kiss (Television Series)

Rose "Smoochie" T. is a huge executive in the fashion world. She chooses her top eighteen outfits for the week. She points out what changes need to be made. She seals each outfit with a "smoochie" or a tea bag kiss. The associates send the changes out. Rose's top eighteen fashion choices affect the stock market.

Rose also sends invitations to people for lunch and dinner. Those people will pay for everything for her if she shows up. If you have been rude to her . . . well, that's your prerogative.

Fashion Kiss was one creative way that my mania took my art work and my thoughts and put them all together.

Paul's Visit

My friend Paul from Toronto visited me in Winnipeg after my parents and I returned from L.A. I had him so convinced I wasn't bipolar that he even argued the point with my mom for more than two hours. He kept saying, "But Sandra isn't ill." My mom said he wouldn't let up. When Paul helped me fill out part of my twelve-page psychological test, I told him on more than one occasion, "You can't answer the question like that because they'll think I'm ill." I even showed Paul my tea bag art, but he didn't think it was as good as I did.

One time I asked him, "How do you get someone to change?" I, of course, was talking about identities because I believed people could have up to five identities.

He answered, "You change your hair colour or your clothes."

That wasn't the answer I wanted. Only my manic mind had the right answer.

After Paul left we continued to talk on the phone every day. He was mostly supportive of me and didn't believe I had bipolar because I told him I wasn't ill—which is what my mind told me. Paul was one of the only friends I stayed in contact with while I was ill, although I also spoke on the phone a few times to another friend in Vancouver, a friend who, ironically, I had met through Emma. But I wouldn't talk to or let other people know about my mental illness because my manic mind didn't believe I had one.

The Manic Mind

When my psychosis got worse, Michael, who was both my brother and a doctor, told my parents if they didn't admit me to the psychiatric hospital, he would. So they took me to the psychiatric unit of the Health Sciences Centre. That was my third psychiatric hospital stay, and my mind was not functioning properly.

In my manic mind, one thought spooled another and they carried on in a continuum. One movement from the television elicited another thought. The television was always on in the blue pastel room. One day the television was on CNN. When the guy broadcasting nodded his head, that meant Joe—another patient about five foot ten with dark hair—was my brother, my twin brother, in fact. But then the broadcaster nodded again. That meant no twin brother, but a twin sister instead. No, my older brother had a twin sister *and* a twin brother. Then the broadcaster shook his head no. No, my brother had two twin brothers. That meant there were five of us because the guy on CNN nodded yes to my brother having twin brothers, which made them triplets, and yes to me having a twin brother. My mind had gone astray and was in a manic state.

My mind again told me I was a relationship expert and that I could see who was supposed to be together in the future. I matched up people on television, and I matched up doctors, nurses, and strangers. I got upset when some patients tried to kiss or touch each other. I knew they weren't supposed to be together because my relationship expertise powers had told me. I even tried to pull apart two patients who kissed, but a nurse interfered.

"Why did you do that?"

My shoulders just shrugged and I walked away. Nobody could know about my special powers.

Because my mind told me I had the power to tell who should and shouldn't be together, I still didn't want Emma to get married. In my mind, that wedding was not supposed to happen. She and I didn't talk while I was in the hospital. I wouldn't let my parents tell her I have bipolar because nobody could know and I didn't believe I was sick. Emma had a beautiful winter wedding and I was hospitalized so I wouldn't have been able to make it anyway. I am still sad I had to miss that wedding, but there was nothing I could have done about it. My mind was gone.

CHAPTER 17

Reliving Those Moment

It is not easy for me, even now, to re-live those moments because in order to share everything I went through on these pages, I have to try and put my mind in a manic-like headspace again. I have to go to a place I never want to go again. I have to describe what it is like to feel that way, to think that way, and to remember what I did and why.

I was sick when I was thinking like that, and reliving that way of thinking is very difficult. My mind was off-kilter, and in order to try and describe my mind being like that, I have to go to the depths of my illness. I can't simply say "I did this" because I want to fully explain the feelings and emotions I experienced, and the only way to do that properly is to try and relive those mentally ill moments, no matter how painful and difficult it is.

There are a number of reasons why everything about having bipolar and experiencing a manic episode and being hospitalized is so hard.

1. Stigma

The stigma attached to the illness is the hardest part of being ill. I had hidden behind the illness for years because I didn't want people to know about what I went through and I didn't want to be judged because of it. When I am ill, I think I am not ill, which stops me from getting the help I need. When I am well, the stigma makes me want to hide my illness from other people because I don't think they will understand. I'm afraid they will overlook the illness and tag me as psychotic.

Nobody at my work knows about my illness except for Human Resources, and the only reason they know is because I have had to take leave over the years so I can get well. Most people simply can't understand what it is like to have a chemical imbalance. They don't understand what the mind goes through and how you can switch from normal thinking to a completely different story and back again, and how the two ways of thinking can combine, often making it difficult to know what is truth and what is fiction.

Think of mania as like having a bad dream, only ten thousand times worse. You wake up and you don't know if the dream actually happened or if it was just a nightmare. All these bad images flash through your mind and you feel haunted. Do you call the person who died in your dream or do you just sit there and think? Thoughts race through your mind. What do you do? This is only a small part of mania; most of my hospitalizations lasted for two to three months. On top of that dreamlike image, you are awake for the manic haunting, so other circumstances around you can be added into your story. Some days your story is vile and terrifying like a jail killing massacre, and other days your story is elated and you are in the middle of making a film.

The littlest things can add to your story and are often thought of as signs. My friend told me she was getting a new car so that was a sign we really were going on a giant tour. Or when the nurse Eric, who I called "Erik Estrada," responded by calling me "Sandra Bullock," that meant I was going on tour and going to be famous for sure. Or the guy on CNN, who just by nodding made me believe I had a twin brother. Then other questions surface. Why did my parents hide my twin from me? Why did they only keep Michael and me when they really had five children? There are so many things that add to a manic story.

How does it feel and how hard it is for an individual with a mental illness to survive? It feels worse and is harder than most people think. After an illness it can take so much effort to push yourself to do things. In taekwondo, you have to think about your foot kicking through a board before you can actually kick through the board. After mental illness, I first had to believe I could do things before I was able to push my mind past the obstacles standing in my way. For example, I had to believe I would work again and then I had to push myself to work toward that. I could've just as easily said, "I can't do that," and thrown my hands up in the air, but I never let my mind think like that.

Yes, the stigma attached to mental illness is the worst part about being ill because most people are not able to see the person behind the illness. Most people won't say, "She went through a really hard time." Fortunately for me, "most people" are not my true friends.

2. The people my mind was angry at

It is particularly painful for me to admit that those people my mind was angry at were some of my family and friends. The first time I was hospitalized, I was angry with my parents and told them they couldn't visit me for a couple of days. I thought they had put me into the hospital, when in reality it was the doctors who made that decision after my parents only tried to help me.

Then, during my mania, when I thought I was a relationship expert, my mind was angry with a lot of people. First, I was angry at my mom when I thought she was trying to hospitalize me again. I was at the Health Sciences Centre seeing a different psychiatrist about the booklet of tests I had filled out with Paul, and had managed to convince her I wasn't really sick. But then my parents came in and told her how I really was. Second, I was angry with Emma because despite the fact she and her fiancé were not the right match, they were still marrying each other instead of other people. And third, I was angry with Maggie because she was friends with Emma and was going to allow that to happen by standing beside Emma at the wedding.

The manic mind can make you believe things about those closest to you that you would never ordinarily believe. Reliving those moments of anger are not only painful, but also difficult to make up for when you are well.

3. Confronting how my smart, intelligent mind went astray

Imagine doing well at academics, sports, and music, and then your mind becomes unhealthy for no reason. Your thinking becomes irrational, you do things you wouldn't normally do, you have a ton of energy, you can't sleep, and the story going on in your head only makes sense to you. You're stuck in a hospital, you don't think that anything is wrong, and you don't believe you have a mental illness. Why would something like that happen to you?

Well, that is exactly what happened to me. My intelligent mind went astray and I had to come to terms with that. I tried to dissect it and pick it apart in order to understand all the reasons. I thought I had done something bad in my life and that is *why* it happened to me. But mental illness has nothing to do with how you are as a person or what you have or haven't done. It has to do with the chemicals being imbalanced in your brain.

After a hospitalization and going through illness, your life is turned upside down. Everything in my manic story came crashing down. All the ideas, thoughts, and feelings I had during the course of the hospitalization were gone. I had to face reality, and that was a large kick in the butt. There was nothing good about being ill in the hospital and the experience, other than I lived to talk about it. After being manic all I thought about was for the next year to come and I kept telling myself it was going to be better. Anything would be better than the pain and torment my mind went through.

4. When the only excitement in my day was the next meal or snack

Besides having family and friends visit you in the hospital, the only excitement is the next meal or snack. You know what time the snack or meal is coming and if you aren't in any of the hospital programs such as occupational therapy or gym, there is nothing to look forward to in a day besides food. You are confined to the hospital where visiting hours are strictly controlled.

However unexciting it might have seemed at the time, routine is important for anyone with mental illness. So, in a way, being hospitalized set me on a clear path for understanding more about and managing my illness.

5. Awful memories, thoughts, and experiences

Finally, there are the after-effects, flashbacks, and the shame my manic experiences created in my life. Many things I did when I was manic I would never have done if I was well, such as doing gymnastics in the hospital while wearing a dress. There were awful memories of refusing to take medications and fighting with the staff as they pinned me down to get a needle in my butt.

Many people who have bipolar do not remember what happens to them while they are hospitalized. I am not one of those people. I am able to clearly remember pretty much everything that happens to me, which is why there is so much detail in this book. It is also the reason why I struggle with many of the things that happened to me, especially those things that are the most painful and the hardest to let go of. Some of the memories I have of my thoughts and experiences are so strong it is both a blessing and a curse. Not only do they help me understand what happened to me, but they also feed the shame and sadness I feel about what I did to those I love when I was ill.

Paul's Email

The last time Paul and I talked to each other was when he visited me shortly before I was hospitalized. Despite what my mom had told him, he still didn't believe I was ill, even though the twelve-page psychological test he helped me complete clearly pointed at something going on with me.

In March 2009, after I got out of the hospital, I tried calling him. I hadn't been able to talk to him the entire time I was there, and now he neither answered the phone nor called me back. Apparently he had stopped talking to me and I didn't know why. I thought perhaps I had said something to offend him, and decided to email him instead.

> *Hi Paul,*
>
> *How are you? I am so sorry if I said things that were mean or hurtful or untrue while I was sick. It was never my intention to hurt you in any way, especially since I considered you one of my best friends at that time. I am also sorry that you left me when I needed a friend the most. I was so disappointed that you couldn't even tell me that you couldn't speak to me anymore.......*
>
> *Sandra*

I was very happy when Paul emailed me back, but that happiness didn't last long.

> *Sandra,*
>
> *I'm doing great. So great, that it's scary: how much better can it ever get. I hope you're doing great too.*

Don't be sorry for so many things. Especially the things you shouldn't be.

As for me leaving you when you needed a friend the most . . . I tried harder than you would have done for me to be your friend, but you wanted more, and I couldn't offer that. And I can't offer that now either. I warned you several times, making it clear that these would have been the consequences, but it made no difference and you did things your way. So don't be disappointed by me at all. As a matter of fact, I was disappointed you forced me away. Shame. But that's the past and I don't intend to cry over spilled milk.

Take care of yourself, Sandra

Paul

Looking back now, Paul clearly didn't know about my illness and I don't blame him for that because I never specifically told him about it. I do, however, blame him for the shame he threw my way with his words. He tried to divert the situation and take the blame off himself, but he was wrong. I didn't force him away; he simply didn't understand what was going on in my brain.

As for what I might have said to him about a relationship while I was mentally ill, that would have been my mania talking. I didn't want him or a relationship from him. While I was ill my manic mind must have concocted a story about why we should be together; remember that in my mind, I was a relationship expert and people had multiple identities. If I did say I wanted to be with him, it would have been because he was all I had at the time. The only person I could talk to and the only person who was really there. It had nothing to do with the way I felt; if it had, I would never have left Toronto to go to L.A. Some sign or signal from him might have led me to want a relationship, but at that time my brain had a completely different story mapped out, one that was untrue but at the time so real it was scary.

I am glad Paul is not in my life anymore. He could never have been a true friend. I mean, who announces to their friend, "I'm doing great. So great, that it's scary: how much better can it ever get" when their friend is obviously in some kind of pain. It shows total disregard for what their friend might actually be going through. Fortunately for me, he is the only person I ever lost because of my illness.

Horoscopes

After my third hospitalization I couldn't look at horoscopes anymore. Horoscopes meant looking into the future, and after my manic mind told me I could read the future when I was hospitalized, I didn't want to think like that ever again. I had discussed horoscopes with bipolar individuals in groups I was in and some said that after an episode, they would not look at them or any type of spirituality. After I was well again and my magical fairytale story had disappeared, I didn't want to think or believe in anything those horoscopes told me again. I was afraid that if I thought about the future, I would go manic, so I completely avoided all spirituality. After my third episode, it took me seven years before I could even look at a horoscope again.

Maggie Called

When I got home from the hospital and was functioning well, Maggie called and talked to my mom. Mom insisted I call Maggie back, but I was reluctant. *What if she is angry at me? What if she doesn't want to be friends?* More questions brewed until finally, after a few days, I did call her.

I was sitting on the multi-coloured futon in the basement. The only light was a ray of sunshine that beamed through the small window. My hand trembled as I held the black portable phone. When Maggie answered, she immediately said she was very happy to hear from me. All I could tell her was that I had been ill. I couldn't say what had happened or that I have bipolar. As tears streamed down my face, Maggie listened and was empathetic.

She then convinced me to call Emma. I was afraid to because I had ruined part of her wedding and I couldn't tell her why. I thought about that for a long while, but eventually got the guts to call her. We talked and made up, and again, all I could tell her was that I had been ill.

When I remember those conversations, I still get tears in my eyes. Two of my best friends took me back and they didn't judge me or blame my illness. They loved me for who I was, and to this day I am so thankful and happy that they are in my life.

CHAPTER 18

L.A. Again

All I wanted after my third hospitalization was to go back to L.A. My heart needed to be in that city and to see the Hollywood sign again. I used all my energy to recover, rest, exercise, eat healthy, and get back to L.A. The side effects from my medications didn't allow me to function and live a normalized life, so with my doctor's help I went off them all.

I emailed surfer dude when I felt better and asked if my bike was still there. He said it had been stolen. Not only had I lost my nice designer high boots and long green superhero jacket, but my fold-up bike was also gone. It didn't matter because those items were only material things and my parents taught me that material things can be replaced, but people can't. So I quickly got over it because I knew my friends, family, and health were more important.

Six months after my hospitalization and before I headed back to California, Sheila and I made amends. All it took was one phone conversation. Then I searched high and low for hostels close to where my Meisner acting class was in North Hollywood. None of them matched the cost of surfer dude's hostel.

In August 2009, I flew back to Los Angeles. Sheila picked me up from the airport and I stayed with her in Santa Monica for a few days. I brought her gifts and dinners because she didn't want money from me to stay at her apartment. There was a Meisner school close to where she lived, so I checked it out, but it was too late. The program had already started, and they wouldn't let me in.

Sheila and I both wanted to exercise, so we went to the Santa Monica Stairs. They are two sets of outdoor staircases close to Pacific Palisades. One set is a mix of wood and concrete and as high as an eight-storey building. The other set is concrete and has approximately 188 steps. People go there to sweat and get a good workout. I was motivated by all the exercise going on on those stairs, and Sheila and I had a good workout session. After she left to go to work, I turned on my computer. I looked up acting classes and jobs and sent out resumes and emails.

Landing an Interview

One of the resumes I sent out was for a pharmaceutical sales position to sell infant formulas. The company set up a phone interview, and that led to an in-person interview in Huntington Beach. Sheila suggested I spend the night there instead of driving all the way on the day and being stressed out about both arriving on time and the interview itself. Excellent advice, so I rented a car and drove to Huntington Beach to spend the night. The interview went well, and I waited to hear back from the company.

The Stuntman

I emailed back and forth with Michael Longley, the stuntman from the *Transformers* movie. We decided to get together and met outside the restaurant Barney's Beanery on the Santa Monica Pier. Inside there were multi-coloured thick-striped booths, licence plates on the ceiling, and hub caps on the wall. Michael and I sat at a table as he gave me some tips about how to pursue a stunt career. At first, he seemed hesitant to help me, but after I showed him pictures of me doing taekwondo, as well as backhand springs and aerials from my fitness competitions, he really opened up about the stunt world. As we were leaving, he told me about a stuntmen's bowling event that was coming up and offered to take me to it. I thought that not having a vehicle in L.A. would be a huge issue, but not if people offered to drive you places.

From Sheila's apartment I went to the beach for a few runs. I often ran by the Santa Monica Stairs for inspiration because so many people got their fitness on there. I thought if they could exercise, so could I. My illness had made me gain so much weight because when I was hospitalized, the only thing I looked forward to was the hospital food. Unfortunately, all that extra weight made me feel ugly and self-conscious.

I knew I wanted to be in L.A. My heart had longed for it the whole time I was hospitalized, and I had seen myself there, all self-confident and in perfect shape. But even though I *was* in L.A., it was not the way I envisioned it. Unfortunately, the weight I had gained tore down my self-image. My self-esteem was diminished because of my recent hospitalization, and my mental illness had a huge stigma attached that I had to hide. I was where I wanted to be, but both inside and out I felt unattractive and insecure because of my last manic episode.

Nevertheless, I was determined to continue with my acting training. To attend classes at the Meisner school, I had to get from Santa Monica to North Hollywood. It took two hours on public transportation—I had to take two subways and a bus. To drive that same distance, avoiding freeways, would only have taken twenty-five minutes.

When I got off the subway in North Hollywood I passed a grocery store and walked past the shop with the same old neat antique luggage in the window. I opened the door to the school and met the man with short curly brown hair and a flat cap who taught the class.

When he asked if he could interview me, I said, "I've already done the interview."

Then I reminded him how in 2008 he and his assistant had interviewed me for his school. He remembered the interview, and immediately accepted me into the next session of the Meisner Intensive class, which was starting on September 7, 2009.

Making Other Plans

After leaving the acting school, I walked over to the hostel I had stayed at before. Surfer dude said there was a room available the next day if I wanted it. I was a bit surprised about that, given what happened the last time I stayed there, but I assumed it didn't matter to him. Besides, I already had the feeling Sheila wanted me out of her place, and it made sense to be close the school, so I agreed to take the room.

Since I had to move all my belongings the next day, I had to rent a car. I knew Sheila would not want to drive me to the hostel, so I went to Enterprise Car Rental, which was within walking distance of the hostel. They printed off directions that would allow me to travel to and from Sheila's place without using the highways.

That was the last night I slept on Sheila's pull-out bed. When I left the next morning, I took my suitcase and backpack, some groceries, and two old couch pillows that Sheila gave me to sleep on. Pillows at the hostel cost money.

Instant Shame

Later the next day, I drove to the hostel where I dropped off my luggage, the pillows Sheila had given me, and the groceries I bought, returned the car to Enterprise, and walked back to the hostel. The first day I was there I met a few people, including a Guyanese guy named Trevor. He stood about five foot seven, had a medium build, wore baggy pants and larger sized t-shirts, and had cornrows and facial hair.

That night Trevor invited me to surfer dude's house, along with some other people from the hostel. Before we left, he used the hostel's portable phone to tell the dude we were all on our way over.

When Trevor listed off the names of those who were coming with him, the dude interrupted him at my name. "She can't come to my house."

The way Trevor looked at me when he got off the phone, I instantly knew. “He said I can’t go, right?”

Trevor nodded his head. “He said no.”

Immediately I felt instant shame as pain swelled in my chest. And then a whole lot of questions started swirling in my head. *Was he not letting me go to his house because of my illness? Was he afraid of me? Had I done something to him? Did he think I would destroy his house and go crazy? Or had he stolen my fold-up bike, boots, and coat, taken them to his house, and didn’t want me to see them?*

The questions kept running over and over in my mind, but there were no answers. The dude made me ashamed of my illness and ashamed of my life. And that made me very uncomfortable about being at the hostel. *Why had he let me have the room? Was it because I was asking in person and he didn’t have the courage to say no? Was it that he only wanted my money?* That hurt my self-esteem even more. I hid in my room that night while everyone else partied over at his house. It was the worst way to start off my new living arrangements.

Healthy Diet

The next morning I decided to forget about surfer dude and focus instead on taking care of myself and eating properly. Before I returned to L.A., I had already lost ten pounds from hard exercise and a healthy diet that was recommended by my psychiatrist, and I wanted that to continue.

As part of a well-balanced diet at the hostel, I made oatmeal pancakes with egg whites, cottage cheese, oatmeal, cinnamon and vanilla extract. All the ingredients were mixed together and then fried to pack a protein punch. They were delicious, especially topped with yogurt and berries. I would fry up enough pancakes for a few days, store them in the fridge, and zap them in the microwave in the morning. That recipe came from my fitness days when I struggled to eat egg whites or oatmeal or cottage cheese by themselves. Instead, someone told me about the idea of combining all the ingredients into pancakes, which was a much tastier option.

Luciana

A couple of days later, despite my best efforts, I was still feeling bad about surfer dude not inviting me to his house. He had made me question my life and feel like I was a bad person because of my illness. But then something happened that made me forget all about him.

Luciana and I met across the huge wooden dining room table at the hostel. For some reason we were instant friends. Our souls connected in such a way that an outsider would think we had known each other for years. Remembering Luciana now makes me very sad because she lives too far away and we hardly communicate.

Luciana had tanned skin, freckles, chin-length black hair, and brown eyes. She had the cutest Castellano Spanish accent, especially when she would say, "Noooooo ummmm?" in an upward pitch. She grew up in Cesantes, Spain, three hundred and seventy-two miles from Madrid, which is where the medieval poet Mendinho was from. Luciana had a real sense of style, and when she lived in Spain, she used to dress all of her eight girlfriends. Occasionally she helped dress me as well. We both loved accessories because of how they could transform an outfit. Luciana was ahead of U.S. fashion styles by at least two years.

Not only was she a great stylist, but she was also a great cook. She could make a mean Spanish omelette with only a few simple ingredients—eggs, potatoes, and oil. That doesn't sound like much, but if you tried it, your mouth would salivate for more. She shared the omelettes with others in the hostel, often making two or more because everyone gobbled them up so quickly.

Whenever I smell potatoes frying or hear the song "Empire State of Mind" by Jay Z featuring Alicia Keys, I think of Luciana. The potatoes because of her delicious omelettes, and the song, particularly the beats and the energy reminds me of a Halloween party we bought tickets to from some guy we met after dark on the Santa Monica Pier. We weren't planning on going out that night, but decided to on a whim. That song was playing at the club during the night and I sang it to her. The event itself was fairly ordinary, but because Luciana was there, it was the best.

She was a great friend. She always had my back, and in many ways she took care of me. She looked out for me while I was sick with the flu. She told me to move on from a guy who was no good for me. She helped me pick out an outfit when I tried to win a date with Ryan Seacrest. And those were only a few of her special qualities. She was a wonderful person who touched my heart then and still does today, even though we rarely see or talk to each other.

A Date with Ryan Seacrest

One sunny afternoon Luciana and I were on Hollywood Boulevard when a brunette woman approached us and said, "Ryan Seacrest would like to make people's dreams come true."

I wanted to say something funny, but the only words that came out of my mouth were, "I want a date with Ryan Seacrest."

The brunette smiled a little, then asked me to go for an audition the next day. She told me I could ask for anything I wanted—a reality show, a car, anything. I only wanted a date with Ryan.

Before going back to the hostel, we found a place to buy poster paper, and that night I made a poster with a slogan to win a date with Ryan Seacrest. Because I also wanted to go to Santorini, Greece, I thought, *Why not combine the two? If you don't ask, you don't get, right?* Honestly, I would have settled for a cup of coffee with Ryan Seacrest, but I was dreaming big. I googled the cost of everything for a trip to Santorini, and wrote something like:

> Two tickets to Santorini, Greece $1,800
> Dinner at a sunset restaurant $562
> Wardrobe styling $10,000
> A date with Ryan Seacrest.......
> PRICELESS.

After the poster was finished, Luciana helped me pick out my wardrobe for the next day. I tried on many different outfits, and in the end what I wore was half mine and half Luciana's. Her shorts, my black top, her scarf, and my shoes. Our clothes together totally worked, but I still felt ugly from the weight gained from my last manic episode.

The next morning Luciana and I travelled two hours by bus to get to the audition. I had the poster in my hands and was ready to win that date, but during the audition my nerves got the better of me and my hands and voice trembled. They could tell I was nervous, and yet they still asked, “Are you nervous?” Let’s just say my dream of a date with Ryan Seacrest was shattered, and I never even got a call from him to go out for coffee. So I moved on.

Luciana and I were both in Hollywood to pursue our passion of acting. She was one of the only people who understood what my dreams were in life. There was no pretending around her because she had the same dreams I did. We took classes at different schools. She took acting at the same school that threw me out in 2008. Every day after class, we shared our days with each other.

CHAPTER 19

Life is What Happens When You are Busy Making Other Plans

The first day of my Meisner acting class started on September 7. It was an intensive class that ran Monday to Friday from 4:00 to 7:00 p.m., with at least an hour of practice afterward every day. There were nine of us in the class, three of whom had already completed the two-year program and were just there for a refresher. My Meisner instructor was Barry, the same guy who interviewed me back in November 2008. I liked how he walked and talked during class to keep us engaged.

One of the first things Barry told us that evening in a serious loud voice was, "Acting is the ability to live truthfully under the given imaginary circumstances." That really made me think long and hard. Whatever circumstance you are given, either on stage or on set, you are to live as truthfully as possible. My mind had never comprehended acting in that way. Before I heard those words, acting had been about scenes, dialogue, characters, and scripts. Living truthfully made acting seem so much more realistic.

Barry made me want to be powerful and confident. He would stand up on the stage or against the brick wall and empower us to be better. He would say, "Meaningless words that take the power out of you, such as like, probably, guess, kind of, sort of, maybe, don't know. Fuck them! Replace them with meaningful words such as I can, I am, I will." That concept made me think not only about acting, but also about life and how you should stay positive and have a positive approach.

Looking back now, there were so many lessons Barry taught us about acting that applied to everyday life. After every class we came out with a new concept, a new life lesson, or a new way to think and approach life. Barry reminded us, "Life is what happens when you're busy making other plans." That is so true when you are on stage in a scene, and so true for my life. He also taught us to live by our instincts. He would say, "Go to your animal instincts." That taught me strength in my acting, and to never give up.

One day, he used the youngest student in the class—a sixteen-year-old boy—to demonstrate the combination of strength and instincts. The boy stood on stage in a martial arts horse-riding stance, and Barry yelled a martial arts *ki-hop* every time he had to punch. The student punched with his left hand and then his right as Barry yelled and directed him. Soon the student had tears in his eyes and his legs shook, but he didn't stop. Barry told us he once held that position for thirty minutes during a martial arts class. He taught us that we have more strength than we know and to always fight for the strength we have. That concept really affected me, like most of my Meisner instructor's concepts.

Ted

My partner at acting class was Ted, Caucasian, six foot four with grey hair, who was lean and in his sixties. I could tell he was lonely because he only ever talked about himself. He pushed my buttons all the time and seemed to be a bit of a bully.

Every day for at least an hour after class we had to practise the techniques we had learned during class. One technique was listening to our partner and repeating exactly what they said in exactly the same way they had said it. Sometimes it was something as simple as "blue shirt." Even though I always listened intently, Ted would tell me I didn't listen. He'd pull on his ear and proclaim, "You have to listen."

Ted was always making some pronouncement or another. More times than I cared to hear, he would say, "You have to have a voice. You can't be afraid to have a voice." That irritated me because I couldn't understand why he kept telling me I had no voice. If having no voice meant having no self-confidence, then he was right, but I didn't need to keep hearing that. I already knew my confidence was shot because of my mental illness. At times that illness caused me to lead a double life because I hid behind it. No one in Hollywood was allowed to know about my illness, so I never told a soul.

During my manic episodes my mind always left me. Then after the episode I wouldn't talk about my illness or the problems that surrounded it. I suppose in that way I didn't have a voice because I wouldn't talk about the illness, but that was because of the stigma associated with it. That stigma caused another layer of complexity. It was hard enough to function with a mental illness, but when you add in the stigma, it made me give up hope. My mind and heart were still bruised from the pain of the last episode, and because that pain was bottled up so tightly and so deeply, it was too hard to release.

My mind was always concerned about what *other* people would think, but it should have just focused on me. I worried about the stigma and the judgements from others. What I really needed was to live in the present and to have a voice, but the present was too hard to focus on when the past was mind-bogglingly ugly.

My Illness Destroyed My Self-Worth

The second day of class, Barry had me stand on stage and introduce myself. He wanted to know the reason for my lack of confidence—I think he actually used the words shyness or quietness—and what had happened to cause that.

As I stood on stage with my hot-roller curled blonde hair bouncing off my shoulders and just a tiny bit of make-up on my face, all I could say was, "Many things."

He pressed for more. "What was the pinnacle moment? You have to figure that out."

Of course the pinnacle moment for me was my illness. It haunts me, it deludes me, it has debilitated me, and at times in my life it has sucked out my self-esteem and my self-confidence, and ruined many days. If I could escape the illness or choose not to have it, I would. Many people do not understand how I have suffered or the complexities I have gone through, and many people can't understand the pain and suffering the illness had created in my life.

Childhood Moment

While I stood on that stage, unable to share the thoughts about my illness, I was certain my acting teacher could see what my lack of confidence had done to me. When he spoke about childhood and learning to go to your animal instincts, my mind went back to the moment in grade four when there was a confidence that completely surrounded me. I was about to enter a gymnasium where the provincial gymnastics championships took place. I walked past the other competitors and was cocky and confident because of my gold-medal win from the previous competition that year. That was the confidence I hoped to use on stage to act. Unfortunately, I could only *remember* that confident childhood moment, not *recreate* it; my heart was too broken from my illness to be self-confident. My mental illness had eaten my self-esteem for breakfast and my Meisner instructor knew that within moments of meeting me. If my goal was to act, I needed to know how to get my self-esteem back.

After class, Ted and I practised Meisner techniques in a lush green park that was close to the school. As I strolled back to the hostel that night, my mind was thinking about many things, particularly that girl in grade four standing on top of the podium with a gold medal around her neck. The girl who was ready to take on the world. I remembered the handout they gave us during gymnastics that read, "If you can imagine it, you can achieve it. If you can dream it, you can become it." There was no name or anything else on the handout, only the quote. I so badly wanted to be that actress who stepped on stage, who was confident, who could handle anything. I had dreamt about it, now I wanted to become it. Become it and you will be done with your search, which means if you become what you always wanted to be, professionally or personally, you will stop looking because you will actually be doing it. In other words, do what you want and love it.

An extension of the verbatim technique we had to rehearse was a scene that included an activity. The activity could be juggling, colouring, bouncing a basketball, playing a guitar, doing a puzzle, or whatever we wanted. During the scene, the person doing the activity had to be in the room for about two minutes before the second partner entered. Then that person had to repeat verbatim whatever the person doing the activity said.

The biggest challenge for Ted and me with that exercise was finding a suitable space to rehearse. I didn't like going over to his house because he talked so much about himself that I never thought I would ever get out of there. The nearby park wasn't always convenient, so then we tried the outside patio behind the hostel. One time, Ted was doing the activity, which was writing cheques to pay his bills. When I entered the scene, I listened and then repeated whatever he said. We barely got started when the dark haired guy and his girlfriend who lived in the bedroom right next to the patio complained we were too loud and asked us to stop.

After that, we rehearsed in my room at the hostel, partly because it was the only room in the hostel quiet enough for us to practise, but mostly because I felt comfortable there. He, however, did not. When I asked why not, he said he didn't like being in the three-person shared bedroom alone. *It's only for two minutes, Ted, but whatever.* I still think it was just an excuse not to have to do an activity. During the times we practised I did eighteen compared to his three or four. When I think back now, maybe Ted just didn't have any ideas. Coming up with many varied activities for acting class wasn't always easy, especially when I didn't have access to a car to go and buy the necessary materials.

Ted drove me nuts, and every night at the hostel, I had a story to share about him or his antics or the rude words he said. It might have worked better for us if he didn't talk and talk and talk about himself.

The next week at school, I brought a few things from the hostel for my activity. When it was my turn to do the scene, I walked up on stage and took each item out of my backpack. On the wall, I hung a black dress with white Asian silk fabric around the chest, and placed a mirror, make-up and chopsticks on the short brown table. Then I opened my computer and clicked on a photo of a geisha girl. As I looked at the photo and into the mirror I started to paint my face. I was applying the make-up when Ted opened the door and entered the scene. As soon as he saw me, his mouth dropped wide open, surprised—shocked?—at the geisha doll idea I had created. Dialogue passed back and forth between us, but unfortunately, because there were others who had to do their scenes, we didn't have time to finish ours that day.

Afterward, Barry walked over to where I was still sitting on the stage in front of the mirror. He looked at all my props, and then looked me in the eyes. "Where did you come up with this?"

"I just thought of it."

"And what were you going to do here? Apply your make-up and get into costume?"

"Yes."

He smiled his approval and walked away.

I was very proud of myself that day.

In the last two weeks of class, Barry taught us how to fill up with emotion. We were supposed to practise that both on stage and at home, and I practised so much I was emotionally drained.

Because at first it was so hard to make myself cry, I asked the other students, "How do you do it?"

An attractive gay guy named Mike with green eyes and dirty blonde hair spoke up. "When I went home for Christmas after taking the program two years ago, I had to reach out and touch everyone to make sure they were really there. That's because in my mind I had killed off everyone in my family."

I just looked at him. I knew I couldn't do that. If I were to cry it had to be realistic, something that personally affected me. I couldn't trick my mind to believe something had happened if it hadn't. Which is ironic because when I am manic, in my mind I can do anything, even fly.

Tears My Teacher Loved

Near the end of that class I waited in the backroom of the theatre until it was my time to go on stage. I knew my instructor wanted tears—he called it filling up with emotion—so I had to think of something that would make me cry.

I visualized my first two phone calls to Emma and Maggie after my third hospitalization. In my mind I was sitting on the brightly coloured futon in the dark in my parents' basement with the black portable phone shaking nervously in my hand. I was afraid I had lost two of my best friends. My voice was trembling and I was on the verge of tears as I said, "I'm sorry for not talking to you." The reason I hadn't talked to them wasn't because of them or me; it was because of the vile place my mind had been in.

My heart hurt to think about my friends who I'm certain would have helped me through the illness, would have helped me while I was ill, and who wouldn't have passed judgement, but who were not there for me because of the simple fact that I didn't let them know I was sick. As a result, they never knew what that vile illness had put me through, or about my painful time in hospital when my very sick mind turned me against them. Mental illness is so debilitating in the way it damages your relationships. And as my mind visualized all those terrible feelings, my emotions were released.

When the door swung open on stage, a stream of tears began to run down my face. Even if I had wanted to, I couldn't tell the acting class the real reason behind those tears because of my fear of the stigma surrounding my illness. So I was the only person in the whole theatre who knew the real reason for those tears—and my Meisner teacher loved them. He was so proud, and not just because I cried when I entered the scene. I know that because I heard Barry say to his assistant, "How does she know how to cry when she enters? That's something we don't teach until the second year."

In the last week of the Level One course of the Meisner Intensive program, we changed partners. That was a happy day. In my mind, Ted was a lonely old man who took his hardships in life out on anyone he could. An African American student in the class who ended up with Ted as his partner came up to me two days later and said, "I don't know how you worked with him for so long." Verification that I wasn't the only one Ted got to.

Mike was my partner for the final scene, and given his previous Meisner training, he made me take my acting to another level. Every time he stepped on stage my eyes were glued to him for the entire performance; he was super interesting to watch. He made every scene look fascinating, even the one where he glued a plate back together. The final scene that we performed together uplifted me and made me feel incredible. After the first run, Barry asked me to do it again, but to talk louder. Normally, I am a very quiet speaker and never raise my voice, so on the next take it seemed like I was yelling my lines, but I wasn't. By the time I was finished, I felt powerful, like I had learned to be a better actress. Barry told Mike and I that we'd had a good performance.

Although Level Two was starting right away, my mind couldn't handle going straight into another intensive Meisner session. The whole process had been difficult emotionally, and the prospect of even more intense study was daunting. Also, I was still struggling with the strain of having Ted as a partner through the first course. I know you should never let anyone stop your dreams, but he enjoyed picking on people, and I was vulnerable because of my recent hospitalization. And teaching myself to cry had drained me even more because it brought up pain from the past. I never knew how to deal with my illness before; it just lingered. It was something that made me lose self-confidence and brought me down because I had to keep it hidden. I was ashamed. Finally, I was never comfortable living at the hostel and having to see surfer dude almost daily, the same guy who had rejected me and embarrassed me.

So instead of finishing the Meisner program, I decided to leave California, devastated about not being able to stay in L.A. to pursue my passion when it was right there in front of me. Even now, that deeply saddens me, but I know my mind, body, and soul were still wounded from my illness and it was the right decision at the time.

CHAPTER 20

Pharmaceutical Sales

I got back to Winnipeg on November 10, 2009, and a few days later, I received a call from the pharmaceutical company that interviewed me during the first week of September. They left a message on my US plastic cell phone. I was able to retrieve the messages from Canada but I couldn't talk on the phone. They wanted me to attend a second interview in L.A. Apparently the woman who first interviewed me in Huntington Beach quit soon afterward, and since nobody was hired for the sales position at that time, they were following up on applicants who had interviewed well the first time round. A sales job would have been great for me and allow me to continue pursuing acting and stunts. After I called the pharmaceutical company to set up the interview on Monday November 30, I called Sheila to see if I could stay with her on the weekend.

When she answered the phone, she initially sounded happy to hear from me. But after I explained about my interview and possible job, she sounded jealous. Something about the perks of the job completely changed the tone of her voice.

So what if I would get a car? You will still have made more money than me.

Then I said to her, "It's not a problem if I can't stay with you, but please let me know as soon as possible so I can make other arrangements."

That was the Tuesday. On the Friday night before my early morning flight the next day, Sheila phoned to say I couldn't stay with her that weekend because she was working and wasn't sleeping well.

Fine, but why the hell couldn't you have told me that on Tuesday?

Several calls later, I found a hotel and made arrangements for a rental car. More stress in my life I didn't need. That Sheila changed everything around at the last minute really upset me. She knew the pharmaceutical interview was very important to me, and her sudden change of plans was not how one good friend should treat another.

I arrived in L.A., picked up my car, and headed to the hotel. The interview wasn't until the Monday, but I didn't want to arrive and go straight to the interview. Sheila phoned me after I arrived and we talked for a bit, but it was Luciana who I really wanted to see. She didn't ever leave me at the last minute.

When I last saw Luciana, my hair was an auburn blonde colour, the result of a box dye while I was in L.A., but because I wanted to look my best for the interview, I got highlights in Winnipeg before I left. As soon as we met up, she said, "You look good," and I know she was referring to my hair.

Luciana and I hung out for a while and it was wonderful seeing her again.

Sunday afternoon I was back in my hotel preparing for my interview when Sheila phoned. She told me I could come over to her place after the weekend and stay if I wanted, but she had already hurt me so much that I could hardly speak to her.

I arrived early for my interview on the Monday morning. It was at a beautiful hotel in West Hollywood. Two individuals interviewed me separately. One of them, a guy in his forties, told me during an earlier phone conversation that he loved numbers, so I brought a calculator to the interview. I showed him a trick I had learned in a university math class; he hadn't seen that trick before and thought it was pretty clever. He also told me there was usually something wrong with people who went into the field of nutrition, but that I seemed normal. Then he said he didn't know if I would be able to talk to nurses. A funny comment given that my mom was a nurse, I grew up around nurses, talked to them all the time while volunteering 700 hours at the hospital, and often had lunch with Mom and her nurse friends. Still, I suppose there was no way for him to know that, and he certainly didn't know anything about my most recent interactions with nurses.

Sadly, the position wasn't meant to be. The pharmaceutical company ended up hiring somebody internally. After the interview, I spent a week in both L.A. and San Francisco with Luciana. She made everything better and my heart wished she lived closer.

It wasn't until I was on my way to L.A. airport that I sent Sheila a text. I decided I couldn't be friends with someone who cancelled on me like that, and I couldn't be friends with someone who instead of listening to me when I didn't agree with her, would rather I stare out the passenger window and stay silent. *You just don't treat a real friend like that.* To top it all off, according to everybody I talked to, it was more likely she had a guy for the weekend and wasn't working at all. Pfffft. I hopped on my flight and returned to Winnipeg.

Keeping Secrets

Shortly after I arrived home, Emma came to visit. We sat and talked over coffee in my parents' kitchen. We talked about her wedding, and I again apologized for not being there for her. We talked about L.A. and the interview and acting classes. I also told her about the scene in my acting class.

"I was standing off stage preparing for the scene, and when I was ready to start, I knocked on the door. My acting partner answered the door and we immediately started the scene. I shed a lot of tears in that scene because I had been thinking about how I thought I had lost you and Maggie, and how difficult it was to make those phone calls to reconnect with you two." Then I added, "My teacher loved the tears."

Emma simply said, "That's funny he loved them."

When I apologized to Emma that day, I didn't say anything about my mental illness. I didn't tell her I have bipolar, which haunts me and debilitates me beyond belief. I didn't tell her that my mind had gone astray. And I didn't tell her that the only reason I am ashamed of my illness is the stigma associated with it. All I could do was talk about my pain and the tears and hope she would understand.

University, Acting, and Pizza

I began looking for work and spent hours every day scanning the newspapers for something suitable for my skills. With no other options in sight, I decided to return to Boston Pizza, where I had worked several years before slinging pizza and pints. I knew the tips there would be lucrative enough that after a year in the job, I would have the money I needed to return to L.A. and study acting again. I lived with my parents during that time, and hardly spent any money, and because I didn't drink, smoke, or do drugs, my only expenses were paying for university, acting courses, and my cell phone, and the occasional coffee or dinner out with a friend.

The reason I decided to attend the University of Manitoba and study nursing was partly because of the comment made during my pharmaceutical sales interview in L.A.—about whether I would be able to speak to nurses. I didn't actually enrol in the faculty and only took the courses for interest because I thought they would help me land a pharmaceutical sales job and stimulate my brain. In 2010, I completed three nursing courses—Microbiology, Human Growth and Development, and Nursing I—and along with credits from my nutrition degree, I had almost completed the first year of the four-year nursing degree.

Also, I took a stage combat course at the University of Winnipeg and acting classes at Prairie Theatre Exchange. Both schools were in downtown Winnipeg. At Prairie Theatre there was Acting Just for Fun and Advanced Film & TV Acting, each of which ran for five weeks in the spring of 2010, and Advanced Acting on Camera that ran for ten weeks in the fall of that year. Before each class I would memorize my lines and practise my scenes as much as I could. My instructor Ed taught us to feel more and think less. He wanted us to get out of our heads and feel more emotions so our acting would come across as more believable.

That was a time when I seemed to have my life under control. I had a goal and a plan to achieve that goal, and was taking all the necessary steps to fulfill my dream. I was looking forward to what lay ahead, and was certain it would work out the way I wanted it to. However, I didn't know I was about to travel an even darker road than I had ever been before, one that would change my life completely. And so in December 2010, with no way of knowing what was to come, I continued forging ahead, back to L.A., confident I was going in the right direction.

Life can change direction so fast.

CHAPTER 21

Van Nuys Jail

When my dad told me, "We'll be there tomorrow," I hung up the payphone.

They didn't feed me the entire day I was at Van Nuys Station. When a female officer walked by around 4:00 a.m. I told her I was starving. "Can I have some food please?"

She simply replied, "Food will not be served for a few hours."

But a short while later, she magically appeared with two tortillas filled with scrambled eggs. I hungrily ate most of the offering. After that my body curled up in the royal blue body bag. Across from my cell I could see the male criminals, but their faces were blurry. I soon fell asleep.

CHAPTER 22

On the Other Side of the Jail Bars

My parents had left L.A. on January 7, 2011, the night before my arrest. They left because they didn't know I was ill, and that was because of my innate ability to hide my illness. When I am ill I can't tell anyone my mind isn't functioning properly. Even when I am in a psychiatric hospital ward I never tell a doctor or a nurse what my thoughts are. And that is because I suffer from anosognosia and simply don't know I am sick when I am mentally ill.

Eighteen hours after my parents left, they were back on a plane to L.A., worried sick about me. My mom is the most level-headed and caring person I know. Everyone tells Mom their problems because she is calm, quiet, does not judge, and will not talk bad about anyone. She is always there for me and helps see me through any problem I have. Which is why it pains me deeply to know that my illness caused a terrible pain and heaviness in her heart.

When they received my call from jail, they booked the fastest flight they could to get back to L.A. Unfortunately, the fastest way included a ten-hour layover in Vancouver.

At that time, Aunt Laura and Uncle Doug, who lived in Calgary, were vacationing in Arizona. For some reason, before they left, my aunt gave my parents the phone number where they were staying. Because my parents were stuck in Vancouver, Dad called their hotel and left a message to see if they could meet my parents in L.A. and help get me out of jail. When Aunt Laura and Uncle Doug heard the message, they immediately took steps to do as my parents asked.

My aunt is about five foot eight and has beautiful brown eyes, although they sometimes look blue depending on what she wears. She has quite the fashion sense and likes to be thrifty when she can, but you would never know it by her wardrobe. Her nails are usually painted and she is great at organizing. My uncle is a jokester who always tries to make people smile and laugh. He even saved his farts for when my brother Michael was in mid swing at the golf course. That caused Michael to flub the shot. My uncle always wears a watch and has a thing for them, and has thick brown hair. He is very technical and detail-orientated. His ability to decipher and understand legal documents and other written material is incredible. I am sure he learned that ability as a result of working for the government for many years and running his own business. He is often dressed in a golf shirt, whether or not he is on a golf course.

Even their efforts to get to L.A. were initially derailed. My uncle's car had been towed the night before my parents phoned him, and they had to get to the impound lot before it closed so they could retrieve the car. Shortly after leaving the lot, my uncle realized he had left his wallet there. He immediately phoned the staff at the lot, but no one could find it. Bright and early the next morning, my uncle returned to the lot and, without the help of anybody who worked there, found his wallet on the desk inside the office. After that debacle, my aunt and uncle drove for six hours to get to L.A. in time to meet my parents.

By the time my parents landed in L.A., my mom was frantic about the whole situation. She was truly afraid she would never see me again—not an unreasonable fear, as it turned out, because for days, nobody *could* find me in the system. My parents and my aunt and uncle had breakfast at McDonald's in Burbank, as they did almost every day they were in L.A. It got to the point that the regulars started saying "hello" to them.

The four of them spent many hours every day making phone calls—to the jail, to doctors, to the police—and trying to find me in the system. When they spoke to one of the city prosecutors, they asked him, "Do you realize the situation here?" That prosecutor had no comment.

They also hired a corporate lawyer who had been recommended by my psychiatrist's brother. My parents had to hire him because they were in an unfamiliar country dealing with a system they didn't understand, and they didn't know who else to call. Besides, they were already stressed and anxious about my situation, and needed to get something happening quickly. Unfortunately, that lawyer wasn't a criminal lawyer, which didn't end up helping my case. Despite leaving many messages for him at various times, the lawyer rarely returned their calls and often left them waiting and waiting for a response. At one point during my case, he left town and didn't inform my parents or my aunt or my uncle.

All of those phone calls, some lasting into the wee hours of the morning, were made from the small apartment I rented in Burbank, the same place from which I was going to launch my career in acting and stunt work. The four of them shared the space, with its two beds—a double and a twin—a few pieces of furniture and a tiny cramped kitchen. My aunt and uncle shared the twin bed the entire time they were in L.A. That apartment was incommodious, especially for four adults.

Van Nuys ~~Station~~ Jail–Day 2

The next morning when I woke up, my hands grabbed the corners of the body bag and started whipping it around from side to side, as far as my arms could reach. Then I grabbed one of my Steve Madden boots and filled it with water, just like a canteen in a desert. I knew what I was doing. I wanted the officers to see me drink out of my boot in the hope that if someone saw, they would help me. An officer *did* see me and heard me gargle the water, but she did nothing.

I had to do something else to get their attention. I quickly did an acting/stunt scene where my head "hit" the wall, I had a seizure where my legs trembled, and then I pretended to pass out. I lay by the toilet for at least twenty minutes, but nobody came to help. All I wanted was somebody to care.

When my body rose from the cold grey concrete floor I placed the body bag over the toilet because it was broken and wouldn't flush, and there was feces in it. That was when I started to make up scripts.

In a later session with my psychiatrist, I said, "Funny I did that while in jail."

"Not really," he explained. "It was a form of protection."

Acting and stunts and running lines for scripts was how I protected myself from the horrible jail system. Even though everything felt unsanitary and disgusting, that didn't stop me from creating one script in particular. I called it *Good Will Hunting 2.0*. My acting was in motion. My bare feet stood on the toilet covered with the dark blue body bag, and I took a moment just like my acting teacher Ed told me to do during class in Winnipeg. There at Van Nuys Station I stepped off the toilet and stood still in front of the bars, my eyes moving from the bottom right to the top left. Tears welled up in my eyes as I looked through the metal bars. I was taught that the camera picked up everything so after you have done the scene, don't be so quick to finish. Instead, take a moment for yourself because they can always cut from the scene but they can't add.

While I was taking a moment for myself, the female officer stopped outside my cell. "Will you see your parents?"

My parents were back in California, back in L.A., and at the jail. They wanted to see me and talk to me while I was behind bars, but my eyes looked up at her, and I said, "No. I will only see Will." I was in character and nothing could stop me.

I only recall being asked once if I would see my parents, but I found out later that they had asked to see me many times. In fact, although they arrived in L.A. on January 9, they didn't actually get to see me until the 17th or 18th. What made the whole situation even more ridiculous was that after I was transported from Van Nuys Station, I was shuffled around between so many locations that not one of the people I needed to help me knew where I was at any given time. I was completely lost in the system for nine or ten days, and it would take an angel to eventually find me.

On the Other Side of the Jail Bars II

When they weren't at the jail, my parents were in court or meeting the lawyer to discuss my release. Every night after going to the jail, talking to the lawyer about getting me released, and spending time in the courts, my aunt and uncle, who drove my parents around and took care of them, would take them out for a good dinner. They usually ended up at a steak restaurant in Burbank.

My dad called my aunt Miss Stability because she helped keep my parents calm and feel better about themselves; she also helped organize details throughout the days. Every day my aunt and uncle drove my parents to the jail. And every day they had coffee and donuts in a rougher part of town where the servers at the donut house were behind plexiglass. There were pennies scattered all over the floor and the food was served to patrons through a chute.

My parents and my aunt and uncle were there for me the whole time I was in the system, and not once during that time were they able to see me from the other side of the bars.

Van Nuys Entourage

After I worked on my script I stood back on top of the toilet seat and yelled for Ari Emanuel. When you want to be an actress you are supposed to study the industry and the business side of acting. Ari Emanuel was the agent I dreamed of working with. He is Mark Wahlberg's agent. I always imagined he would fight for me, and that is what I wanted—someone to fight for me. The character Ari on the television show *Entourage* is loosely based on him. That day in Van Nuys Station as my legs stood on the toilet, I yelled and yelled and yelled and yelled for Ari so much that they shut the door beside my cell. Nobody could hear me yell anymore because they had shut me out. Even when my mind was astray and I was in a high stress situation, my heart was true to my dreams.

Locked in a Cage

The next day, they handcuffed me and shackled me and took me from my cell to a prisoner transport bus, then to a holding area, then back to a different bus, then locked behind bars in another holding area to the final destination—jail. I don't know where we went or why we were being moved around so much, but I suspect it might have been some form of "diesel therapy" or "bus therapy." That is when troublesome or disruptive inmates are hauled around on buses, sometimes to far-away facilities and incorrect destinations. Whatever it was, it explained why nobody, including my parents, could find me in the system after I left Van Nuys. Every time I was in a holding area (a small building with one room and a tiny jail cell in what seemed like the middle of nowhere) I was locked in a tiny cell while the other inmates got to sit on benches or stand in the otherwise open area.

One police officer I kept seeing in the jail had dark slicked-back hair and dark eyes. My sick mind had concocted a nightmare story about him, and I became very afraid of him. When they took me to the transport bus, I was led down a hallway by a guard. When we walked past that officer, my legs immediately gave out, I fell to my knees, and my body slumped on the ground. I began to cry uncontrollably. Tears streamed down my face and there was nothing I could do about them because the guard continued to keep a firm hold on my still-cuffed hands. In the instant we passed that officer, my mind had flashed to a visual of blood, a rope, and a sixteen-inch double-barrel pistol soaked in blood. I cried because I knew what that officer did to innocent people with his pistol. As soon as the guard lifted me up from the floor and we moved away from that officer, the tears stopped.

The guard then escorted me onto the bus and as I passed a police officer he told me, "You shouldn't do that to my partner. He's a good guy."

"Don't talk to me like that," I said as my eyes starred at him.

He replied, "If you act like that, you are going to die in Alameda."

Two people told me I would die in Alameda. He was the first.

The bus was full of male criminals. I felt uneasy because I thought a couple of the criminals had done terrible things. So when they walked past me on the bus I hawked a big loogie on one of their faces, then I turned and spat on another one. The guard grabbed me and locked me in a yellow-chipped-paint metal cage that was the size of one bus seat and went from floor to ceiling.

I began doing stunts for my prison drama because in my mind, I was going to be on television in the fall. My mind switched back and forth between the prison drama television show and the film *Good Will Hunting 2.0*. My body tumbled upside down and bounced around the cage like a rubber ball. My head whipped around to the ground and my hands broke my fall. My arms flailed and my legs swung widely around the cage. If anyone had seen me through the windows of the bus, they would have only seen my legs flying into the air. But nobody "saw" me and they didn't come to help. Instead they left me cuffed and shackled and locked in a cage.

When the music started playing, I jumped on the seat and started dancing. My mind thought it would be a great scene for *Good Will Hunting 2.0* because it fit perfectly into my script.

As I continued to dance, one of the Caucasian inmates with short bleached blond hair at the back of the bus suddenly yelled, "Woo, shake it, you stupid whore."

That didn't faze me at all. I was in the midst of my script, in character, and didn't care that an inmate had called me a stupid whore.

After I got off the transport bus, a guard escorted me through the tiny holding area where I saw a bunch of female criminals. While my mind was processing that, a door creaked open and they tossed me into another dirty, dark, and dingy jail cell, the only one in the holding area. When they shut the door behind me, the bars vibrated. I was locked up again while every female but one was on the other side of the bars, either standing or sitting on benches.

The only other person in the holding area jail cell told me, "You'll get off easier on drug charges than if you plead insanity."

It sounded like she knew how to work the system. In hindsight, I think she was right.

Another girl sitting on one of the benches outside cried out that her stomach ached. She had a dirty blonde ponytail and was clearly in agony. I got upset when three Asian women went to help her; the women looked like they worked in the jail system but not as jail guards. I was upset because in my manic mind the girl was only in pain because she had swallowed a cocaine bag, and I didn't like that at all.

My fists clenched the bar and I cried out, "Why are you helping her? She swallowed a bag."

In the midst of my manic episode, my mind went back and forth from undercover cop to stunts to practicing my script. Even now as I write my story, it is painful to remember everything that happened back then and to relive it over and over again. Once you get inside the system, nobody tries to help get you out. A mental patient can be thrown in jail without the support they need, and the system does nothing to *get* them the help they need. Esther Lim, the Jails Project Director at the American Civil Liberties Union in Southern California, was right when she said, "The jail had a history of not providing adequate medical care or mental health care" (Balsamo, 2017).

After waiting in the holding area's tiny, grungy cell for what seemed like forever I was put on another bus for some more "diesel therapy" before I arrived at a different destination. After I got off the transport bus, I thought I had been taken to a men's jail because as the guards escorted me through a hallway of cells, I only saw three female criminals. While my mind was processing that, a door creaked open and they tossed me into another dirty, dark, and dingy jail cell.

On one side of the cell was a mint green metal square-shaped bar that looked completely out of place. Even though I wasn't sure what it was used for, I figured out how to flip backwards over the bar and land on my feet. My gymnastics background made that easy for me.

Suddenly, out of nowhere, six male guards came into the cell. They didn't say why they were there or where they were taking me, but I knew I didn't want to go with them. When I was hospitalized in 1996, it took four people to carry me to places I didn't want to go. Past hospitalization experiences had taught me how to protect myself by making my body weight dead. Between that and taekwondo, my mind had learned how to put up a fight.

While I swung my body and battled them in defense, those guards struggled to pick me up and carry me through the halls of the jail. As we passed a line-up of criminal men, some of their jaws dropped. I didn't think they would be scared of anything, but they were scared of me.

Those guards never told me where they were taking me, and by trying to defend myself, I was simply standing up for what I believed was right. In that system, they didn't treat me with any dignity or respect when they locked me in cells and cages like I was some kind of cooped-up animal. They didn't try to help me. They didn't explain anything. They didn't give me choices. They just told me I would die. My refusal to cooperate was one of many on my part while I was in the jail system. My parents taught me to stand up for what you believe is right, and even though my mind was off kilter, there was a reason for my resistance—survival. When someone is mentally ill, you shouldn't psychologically debilitate them. You should treat them fairly. You should show them some kindness.

On the Other Side of the Jail Bars III

On the same day the guards tried to take me to the courtroom, my uncle went to court with my mom. My uncle handled most of the legalities when it was too difficult for my parents.

My uncle approached the bar and asked, "Can I speak to the judge?"

The judge waved my uncle over.

My uncle advised the judge. "Sandra has a medical history and it can be substantiated."

The judge looked at my uncle and said, "I will prepare an order that directs that she receives medical treatment, possibly the 5150."

A couple days later my family went to the courthouse to find out what was going on. They had lost contact with my whereabouts because I was being shuffled around so much. My uncle saw the first city prosecutor and advised him what was going on. The city prosecutor then took my uncle through the judges' chamber and into the courtroom to speak to the judge directly. The city prosecutor interrupted the trial so my uncle could speak to the judge. It was a different judge than he saw the first time.

My uncle approached the bench and asked the judge, "Do you realized what is going on here?"

"Yes, something is wrong here," the judge replied.

Something *was* wrong. Terribly wrong. I should have been in a hospital. I was not supposed to be behind bars in a crooked jail system. I was not a criminal.

The judge asked the court reporter to straighten things out. That is when the order to transfer was initiated.

The judge said to my uncle, "Under the circumstances I believe that she should've never been charged."

The judge was not impressed with the legal counsel I had and told my uncle, "Next time, sir, hire a *criminal* lawyer."

CHAPTER 23

Courthouse Jail

While all that was going on, I succeed in preventing the guards from taking me where they wanted me to go. My resistance saw me locked in a different cell with cement walls and a solid door that had a small window covered with bars. I was completely shut off from the world. The only time the small window was opened was when the guards wanted to talk to me.

I stood in that drab, cold cell for hours and yelled every time I heard someone talking. As soon as I heard a voice outside, I would immediately yell, "Beat it" or "Next." That was a joke in my mind because a friend of mine from Vancouver had done it in Mexico when we tried to hail a cab. I would ask, "How much?" in Spanish and when the cabs tried to rip us off, my friend yelled, "Beat it" or "Next." When I wasn't well, my mind looked for humour wherever it could. I wondered, *Is my yelling a form of entertainment to them? Am I their next joke to toy with?* After yelling for hours, I did stunts for my prison drama coming out in the fall. Cross block, elbow, kick, throw, choke, punch. I choreographed fight scenes for hours in that dirty, dingy cell with paint chips and graffiti.

What I didn't know was that my cell was in the same building that housed the courtroom where my uncle and my parents had been relentlessly trying to secure my release, as well as to ensure the proper treatment for my illness.

Another Snake

At one point, a jail guard showed up at my window. I recognized him from the short time I had been in the system. I had learned not to like him, and certainly not to trust him. Even in my manic state, I knew his appearance at my window meant he would coerce me into doing something I didn't want to do.

He stood there for a moment or two and then told me to show myself to him. When I said I didn't want to, he pleaded, "Please? For me?"

It was against my morals and against how I was raised, but for some reason my mentally ill mind told me to slowly push aside my pink lace bra. I revealed part of my right nipple. As if that wasn't enough, the disturbed jail guard told me to go to the bench and show him the rest of me. I slowly turned, walked to the bench that hung from the wall, and pulled down my underwear and pants. I exposed my ass and immediately felt disgusted and inadequate.

As a reward, the guard left me a glass of water.

Everything I did for that pervert was against my morals and contrary to how I was raised. My dignity had been taken away and my heart ached with pain to the utter core. I felt pure shame and was filled with regret. Why my mentally ill mind decided to show myself to such a sick pig that day is beyond comprehension. That incident has been discussed many times in therapy, and each time my eyes filled with tears and I wept with embarrassment. That situation harpooned my heart, and for years afterward, I hid my body from shame and concealed my soul. I wore layers of clothes or baggy clothing to hide from that nightmare so I would never go back there again. At some point later, I wrote down my thoughts about that experience:

> The shadow from my heart makes my life turn grey,
>
> When I think of you my head just turns away.
>
> My life used to fill with this light, this sense of spark,
>
> Now my life is like loneliness living in the dark.
>
> Each day now my life passes by full of
> endless sorrow,
>
> For it is hard to face the mirror and try and live
> for tomorrow.
>
> Traumatic flashbacks keep entering my mind more
> and more,
>
> My realization about the whole situation makes the
> tears pour.
>
> You caused me so much anxiety and trauma in my
> life that won't go away,
>
> For years I covered my body and soul just to be able
> to continue in the light of day.
>
> What you did to me haunts my existence,

But if I were to try and tell you, you would never listen.

You care about being tough in front of your co-workers,

All I think of you is as a dirty, gross jail guard lurker.

You are a bottom feeder that prays on the ill,

The way you looked at me when I exposed myself could kill.

Those beady eyes and disgusting demeanor,

Too bad we couldn't put you in front of all of the females in jail and you have to show your wiener.

You made my life so empty, so meaningless, so hurt,

I feel like you played with me like a child and it's dirt.

The healing, trauma, and torture I had to go through to get to where I am today,

It is amazing what I have accomplished with all the darkness you put in my way.

Therapy has taught me that the jail guard should be the one who is ashamed, not me. After he left, I took my anger about what had happened and fought my way through it by kicking, punching, blocking, and choking. Then Lucy Liu, or so I called her because of her beautiful dark, glossy hair, glasses, and put together appearance, opened the small window of my cell door. "Your uncle has sent me to talk to you," she explained. She was the assistant to the lawyer my parents had hired.

My brain couldn't fathom what she was saying, and at first I just stared at her. What is going on? There is no way my uncle could be in California. He lives in Canada. This can't be real.

I was so angry about what had happened and confused by her words that I told her if she came any closer I would smash the clipboard she was holding over her head. After she left, I started doing stunts, but it wasn't enough to banish the shame of the exposure that still covered my soul.

How is it possible that a system designed to house the mentally ill has no way to identify and punish demented and perverted jail guards? And how often does it happen that people like that prey on the sick and the vulnerable who are supposed to be under their care? I would love to know if that guard ever got caught. Certainly the $65,000 or $70,000 he was paid a year could have been put to much better use.

The Axe Kick

It was a different guard who took me from my cell to see my incompetent lawyer. The guard put me in a large, open room with a glass divider. Before I talked to the lawyer, I did taekwondo kicks around the room. I knew I was in jail and I thought my kicks would demonstrate my toughness.

When the lawyer walked in, I sat on the closest stool and my hand grabbed the receiver of the phone. The lawyer talked to me on the phone from the other side of the glass. My parents had sent my glasses with him as a sign for me to know they were there, but my mentally ill mind didn't get the signal. I glared at the lawyer and squinted my eyes as I told him, "You're a crook."

In my manic mind he had stolen money from my dad, and my hand soon hung up the phone on him.

When I got up from the stool, the lawyer left and I practised more taekwondo kicks in the room. Then my eyes glanced across the hall where the jail guards sat in an area covered with plexiglass. A guard with a shaved head, dark eyes, and tanned skin motioned for me to kick, and then he pointed at the other guard. My mind would never have thought to kick a guard, but because shaved head guard told me to, as soon as I stepped through the doorway my right leg went up for a jumping axe kick. That is where you kick your leg straight up in front of you, high above your head while jumping and bring that leg down like an axe.

My leg kicked six feet in the air and just skinned the face of a tall, overweight Caucasian guard. He immediately grabbed me, turned me, grasped my hair, and smashed my face into the concrete floor. Luckily my chin broke the fall and not my face. My chin split wide open and I lay there with my face on the ground. My body convulsed as tears streamed down my face and blood dripped from my chin.

Still crying, I turned my head just as a girl who had been arrested walked in. She wore street clothes, high heels, and looked like Nicole Richie. My face was so close to the concrete that I was eye level with her heels. When she took off her heels, she had sandwich bags on her feet. *Was that to hide evidence?* That picture is still so vivid in my mind, and so is the pain my chin and body suffered from the abuse I went through.

Eventually, shaved head and another guard drove me in a police car to Sherman Oaks Hospital to get stitches for the laceration on my chin. That those asshole guards messed with me was bad enough, but the worst part was that my mind wasn't mentally sound and I was unable to defend myself.

At Sherman Oaks Hospital I didn't want to get stitches because I was afraid of the doctor. Shaved head guard told me the doctor was okay so I finally allowed him to stitch the wound. All the while, shaved head guard was in the room eating pudding from a small plastic tub. When I told him I wanted one, he got a pudding and gave it to me. I'm pretty sure he did that as a reward for what I had done.

After stitching me up, they took me back to the jail. And after only a glimpse of blue sky from the back of the police car, the "diesel therapy" resumed. While walking from one holding cell to yet another transport bus, I clearly remember one of the guards walking beside me. He commented, "You are too pretty to be in here."

I looked at him and replied, "You shouldn't be hitting on me."

He said, "I'm not," and then he escorted me to the bus.

CHAPTER 24

Alameda

It was nighttime when the bus took me to another institution in the L.A. County jail system. According to the jail medical records, I was taken to the Century Regional Detention Facility (CRDF), an all-female jail system. That facility is commonly known as "Alameda" to the inmates and staff because of the street on which it is located. When I heard someone call it that, I recalled what the guard said about me dying in Alameda.

What I still don't understand is why they took me there because it closes at 5:30 p.m., and when we arrived it was definitely pitch black outside. I suppose they got some special dispensation to do that because my intake form confirms I was admitted at eleven something that night.

In any case, it was yet another reason my parents couldn't find me again and why I remained lost in the chaos of the system.

On the way to Alameda, the bus lights were off and the music was on full blast. When I started dancing, an African American girl behind me shouted, "You've got the groove," and then she started dancing as well. My mind was back in undercover cop mode, and I danced to the music to throw the other criminals off. I didn't want them to know about my undercover work. After I danced, my butt fell into the seat. There were approximately ten criminal women on that bus, one of whom told me, "I've been wanted for ten years."

My mind thought the pinky-red wrist band with a silver circle in the centre that I was given when I got my mugshot had a chip in it that I could use to relay information to those who needed it. So I said into the wristband, "Check one. There is a plane flying overhead that is transporting a criminal charged with manslaughter. Check one. Oh, and the woman sitting behind me has been wanted for ten years."

The African American woman sitting in front of me kept talking about snow trays in Washington. Because I knew "snow" was slang for cocaine, my mind told me snow trays were cocaine on a painting, which is how I thought cocaine was packed and transported. I found out later that a tray is "slang that heroin addicts use for a small square of foil with a piece of heroin on it that has not been smoked off of yet" (Urban Dictionary, 2011). Clearly not something you'd find hanging on a wall.

I decided those two African American criminals knew each other when one said to the other, "Tony asked about you. You know, Tony who owns the store in Tennessee."

I stood up and started moving my body and dancing to the music, which for some reason was turned up extremely loud. At one point, the criminal behind me thought she saw a mouse and stood on her seat screaming out of control. That caused the girl across from me to stand on her seat with her ass in the air and scream. She stood there squeezing her cheeks like she had keistered a load of cocaine in her ass and didn't want it to come out. She had freckles and frizzy dark hair, and one of the other inmates told me her twin sister was also on the bus.

The blonde girl from the holding area was sitting at the front of the bus near the guards. She kept yelling out in pain about her stomach, and then she cried and sobbed. I yelled out to the guard who was helping her. "Leave her alone. She swallowed a bag."

Toward the end of the bus ride when I announced, "Someone is pregnant here," the Hispanic girl in front of me turned and said that she was. I got the "knowing when someone was pregnant" insightfulness from my mom. She used to predict long before they told anyone else when women who she worked with were pregnant. Somewhere on that bus my mom's intuitive pregnancy sense came to me.

Then the other Hispanic girl with long dark hair who sat beside the pregnant one looked at me with daggers in her eyes and angrily declared, "You are going to die in Alameda." She didn't swear, talked perfect English, and didn't use any slang words, but she was trying to intimidate me so she would look cool in front of her inmate friends.

I chirped up and told her, "Get your lingo straight because you don't know how to talk right."

We were escorted off the bus and directed into Alameda. I had been told twice that I was going to die in that place, so I wasn't very happy about being there. Some of us were put into a large open room, while others were put into cells. In the room with me was a criminal who was tall and large, and had dark short hair, which made her look more like a guy. My astray mind decided she was the criminal I talked into my wristband about on the transport bus, and that she had been brought in for manslaughter. I didn't understand why they put only one handcuff on her, while they not only cuffed *both* my hands, but used another three sets of cuffs to strap me to the post of the bench. My wrists were in agony, but I eventually found my way to the floor to alleviate the excruciating pain. I yelled, "I want to be cuffed like her!"

Across from me in a cell was a Hispanic girl with pale skin and blonde hair. She looked terrified. She kept pacing and looking at the manslaughter girl. My eyes saw her take a Kleenex and wipe her gums and then wipe all her fingers one by one. From where I sat, it appeared that she was hiding evidence. Then they opened her cell and let her walk out scot free. *What is going on in here?*

Twenty minutes later, a woman with frizzy, bleached-blonde hair walked by pushing a large grey plastic bin on wheels. She looked like she smoked a pack an hour. She obviously worked inside the system and rammed the bin into a wall. My mind told me she had just dumped the bones and carcasses of all the people who had been murdered in Alameda. I imagined a massive killing spree.

Then I saw a green drug company folder on the wall close to the door beside the desk where the guards sat. I thought I could read the word Novartis on the folder, and after women were injected, I thought that was where all the paperwork was stored about the pharmaceuticals used on them. My mind told me that drug company supplied all the drugs to put criminals to sleep because people died in Alameda, just like what I'd been told was going to happen to me. When a woman on a stretcher to the right of the desk yelled out and someone gave her an injection, her body collapsed inward—confirmation that something bad was going on in that place.

Approximately thirty women arrived on two busloads at Alameda that night. The guards took most of the women in two line-ups to another large open room adjacent to the one I was in. They left me on the floor cuffed in pain; the manslaughter criminal just stood there, looking a bit weird. All of a sudden, she started to yell, "I have to go to the restroom. I have to go to the restroom." When nobody helped her, she whipped down her pants and peed all over the bench right in front of everyone. After that, the guard allowed her to go to the restroom whenever she wanted.

From my awkward and uncomfortable position on the ground, I could see the guards at the front of the lines instructing the criminals how to change into their jail attire. When all the women were finished changing, a Hispanic guard with a long, dark, shiny black ponytail and white nail polish on her long fingernails directed them into two different cells. She asked every third inmate, "How old are you?"

I called out to that guard, "Hey pretty lady. Why are you asking them their age?"

"I subtract five or six years to determine what cell they go into."

My eyes squinted in thought and confusion. "Then why aren't you asking *every*one their age?"

Then she started asking every criminal their age. Strange that she didn't do that until after I questioned her about it. There were many things about the entire system that were seriously questionable.

My astray mind told me to entertain the crowd. So with my body lying on the floor and my hands cuffed to the bench, I pretended to seizure. That was about all the entertainment I could do from the position my body was in. An African American girl with long braided hair inside one of the cells pointed at me. "This shit is so funny it should be on TV." I smiled with my head in the carpet as the guards ignored me.

Long White Fingernails

After all of the criminals were divided into two different jail cells, I was finally uncuffed. Five guards took me into the same large open room where the criminal women had got changed. I thought I was going to die. All five guards pinned me to the wall. One of them kept patting the pocket on her chest by her breast before they frisked me. It was like she had drugs in there that she was going to use to finish me off.

Two of the five guards standing on either side of me had long white fingernails. I don't know if they injected me that night, or whether it was their fingernails digging into my arms, but many times I cried out in pain. They really hurt me and they didn't care. They just called me princess.

"I'm not a princess," I countered as I called out in pain each time they injected me or dug their fingernails in to hurt me.

Two people on two separate occasions had told me I was going to die in Alameda, and that night I actually believed them.

The guards removed all my clothing, my bra, my underwear with blood stains on it—I had just got my period—and put me in a yellow top and blue pants. What I had worked to cover up for years was now uncovered for all the world to see. The L.A. County Jail yellow top and blue pants means you are mentally ill. And that night in that eerie place, the loud, conspicuous, demeaning attire in those gaudy colours screamed to all and sundry that I was insane.

In the Los Angeles County jail system "More than 70% of current inmate population report a serious medical or mental illness upon initial assessment" (County of Los Angeles, n.d.). According to Hare & Rose (2016), that jail is a seven-hundred-million-dollar system, the largest jail system in America, and it needs to find ways to take mentally ill individuals to hospitals instead of incarcerating them. Officers also need help understanding and implementing the 5150 California law to get mentally ill individuals the appropriate medical help they require.

Formaldehyde and the Form

After they had flagrantly exposed my secret to the world, the guards at Alameda re-cuffed me, re-shackled me, wrapped a chain around my body and waist, sat me in a wheelchair, and took me down to a shuddersome basement that stank of formaldehyde. They wheeled me past several offices to an open area where I was evaluated by two different people.

Between 11:26 p.m. and 11:49 p.m., I underwent two evaluations. The mental health counsellor asked me to talk about what I knew of the circumstances of my arrest, and the staff nurse recorded information for their database, including complaints I had about how I was treated.

Then the nurse insisted I sign a form so they could give me any medication they wanted. *If you're going to chain me up, cuff me to a pole, and try to medicate me, why can't you see I need to be in a hospital?*

I recalled my dad telling me never to sign anything you do not believe in or agree with. He said to just stroke a line through the form. It was one of many ways I was taught to stand up for what I believed was right.

I refused to sign the form, which upset the jail staff. Then I asked the nurse what her schooling was. When I am in a manic state and someone asks me lots of questions, I try to re-direct the conversation and ask a lot of questions back. She answered me quietly about her schooling. I didn't hear her. *Can you blame me for not signing the form to overmedicate me?* They had just injected an older lady on a stretcher upstairs and her body collapsed inward. Plus, they put my wrong age on the chart. I hope the individual who was calculating birthdates is not responsible for calculating medications.

There were many ways I protected myself against those jail workers who abused their power. I refused to sign the form to take any medication, I refused to let them overmedicate me, I refused to go to the courthouse, and I used my black belt fighting techniques to defend myself.

After I refused to sign the form they took me back upstairs to a dark area with a bunch of cells. When we reached a set of stairs, they told me to get out of the wheelchair and walk. Instead, I ran up the stairs—surprisingly quickly given the cuffs and shackles—and the guard had to chase after me. When the guard caught me, she put me into a cell, made me place my hands behind my body in tiny openings of the door, and uncuffed me. There were lots of red marks sprayed all over the walls that looked like blood; if it wasn't blood, somebody must have painted red inside the cell. Despite the red accents, the cell was cold, dingy, creepy, and eerie. On the floor under the bed were tiny packets that looked like they should contain ketchup or mustard, but the one my hand picked up was only hair conditioner. Some of the packets were open, others were not.

The lady from the basement tried to get in touch with me in the cell over the intercom system. "Will you take your medication?"

"Pardon me?" They wanted me to verbally sign the medical form.

"Will you verbally agree to take your medication?"

"No," I insisted.

What I really wanted to ask was, *Why can't you just take me to a hospital? I deserve to be treated fairly. Not abused, bruised, cut, and exposed.*

Praying Not to Die

Throughout the night, a guard kept walking by flashing a laser pointer in the cell. That frightened me and made me afraid for my life. The only spot the guard couldn't touch me with the laser pointer was close to the door, so that is where I sat. My knees were folded into my chest and my arms hugged them tight as my voice cried out, "Please, God, don't let me die in here."

In the dark I heard what sounded like sixteen gun shots and a lot of screaming. My mind imagined innocent people being knocked out by the guards' long flashlights and then being choked to death by a rope. The shotgun noises were probably just jail cell doors closing or more inmates arriving, but I couldn't see anything in the black of night.

My mind flashed to the two separate people on two different occasions who told me I would die in Alameda. Given the red marks in the cell, the gunshots, the screaming, the woman who had been injected, the terrifying basement, the formaldehyde, and my treatment at the hands of the uncaring guards, dying in Alameda didn't seem so far-fetched.

My ill mind worked overtime that night. The stench of formaldehyde was tattooed on my psyche and lingered in my brain. Some of the blood stains on the walls had been washed off by the many packets of conditioner that smoothed away the evidence of the killing spree. Bodies were being replaced one by one during the night after the final injections did their job in the eerie basement. Organs were being shipped to other countries on the black market. Criminals walked free while innocent people did time for them. And all the while, my body was curled up by the jail cell door, terrified for my life. It was another sleepless night and my mental state was getting worse. When I woke up the next morning, an African American inmate was hosing off the concrete on the bottom floor of the jail. When I saw the water on the floor, it scared the crap out of me. I was convinced she had been removing all the bloody evidence from the massacre during the night.

Imagine your mind running a frightening story in your head, with shocking images of wild killing sprees. Imagine that nobody can help you, that you are trapped in a jail cell, your thoughts working overtime, terrifying you, making you feeling helpless. Imagine that the only safe place is huddled on a cold concrete floor with your arms hugging your legs and your body shaking as you pray not to die. Imagine all of that and you'll have just a small glimpse of what it is like inside my mind when I am manic. Imagine all of that and then tell me if you think I belonged in jail.

On the Other Side of the Jail Bars IV

Although neither my parents nor my aunt and uncle were able to see me the entire time I was in the system, they were relentless in their efforts to help as much as they could. My dad stayed on the phone late into the night, trying to find a doctor who could see me in the L.A. County jail system. I didn't know at the time, but while I was locked behind bars, my family never gave up and continued to work tirelessly behind the scenes.

Late one night around 4:00 a.m. my dad finally talked to a psychiatrist on the phone who agreed to find out where I was in the system and see what he could do. That doctor instilled hope in the hearts and minds of my family, and ultimately facilitated my release.

CHAPTER 25

An Angel in Disguise

The next morning I woke up alive. When the psychiatrist came to see me, he recorded his initial observations in my chart: "Inmate is very guarded, cautious, displaying manic symptoms. I went to the cell with the Deputy and the inmate was hiding in the corner of the cell, trembling."

Something about the way he spoke to me made me agree to talk to him.

Before that could happen, however, the jail staff took me downstairs. They gave me breakfast on a round concrete table that had concrete bench seats attached. It was right in front of the criminal women in a cell; theirs was located under the stairs directly beneath my cell. I started to entertain again. I cut the banana into my cereal with a spoon. Then I pretended to start convulsing on the bench. An inmate yelled, "She's so funny." After my show I sat on the cold concrete bench alone until a social worker came to talk to me. She had glasses and frizzy dark hair. Because my mind didn't like something about her, I couldn't tolerate her at that time and was rude to her. I also denied having a mental illness.

She looked at me and asked, "Then why would your parents contact the Department of Mental Health?"

"I don't know. I can't speak for them."

When she asked about my mood, I told her, "Those bitches were putting needles in me."

Throughout the interview I attempted to turn the questions around on the social worker and asked her the same questions she asked me. She told me the assessment was about me, not her. It wasn't long before she left.

And then the psychiatrist appeared again. He was five foot eleven with dark blonde hair and a thin build. It seemed to me that there was a bright yellow circular light illuminating from his face. An angel in disguise. He was kind, gentle, and empathetic, exactly how a psychiatrist should be. And he treated me like a human being rather than a caged-up monster. He was the only one who helped me in the system, and was the reason they eventually let me out of jail, although there was still resistance from the system to let me out.

The psychiatrist said, "It would be in your best interest to be compliant by taking your medication. I'm certain it will be a positive factor in your case." Up until then, I had resisted taking medication because I didn't believe I was ill, but he explained, "You have taken these medications before and they will help you again now."

Because he took the time to explain in language I could understand why I needed the medication, I said I would take it the next time it was offered to me.

Then I asked him, "Can I have some paper to write down the story about why I was arrested?" Even in my state of mind, I knew the things that had happened to me weren't right.

I also asked, "Can I have a photographer, please?" I didn't tell him why, but I wanted to photograph all the bruises on my arms and legs so the world would see all the abuse my body had taken from the jail system.

And finally, "Can I get a bra?" I wanted some of my dignity back.

Even though I said I would do what he wanted, I still didn't get anything *I* wanted. According to my chart, that night I was given an antipsychotic medication in wafer form called Olanzapine, and also liquid Lithium, which was the psychiatric medication Lithium in syrup form. Despite what the chart said, while I vaguely remember the wafer dissolving under my tongue, I have no recollection of taking Lithium that night. I was offered medication at least seven times in Alameda; five of which I declined.

Liquid Lithium

The next morning a long-haired Asian lady with fake nails and long fake eyelashes came to my cell.

"What is that?" I asked, pointing to her back.

"Liquid Lithium."

The plastic container strapped to her back contained the medication that was then pumped out through a hose. She handed me a tiny plastic cup of the stuff through the jail bars. I'm not sure why my hand reached out and grabbed the cup that day; probably because I promised my angel that I would.

Most psychiatric medications need to be monitored because they can cause problems if they get too high a level in the blood. So why did they walk around and pump that medication out of a hose? Is one pump a certain amount, two pumps another amount, and three pumps the most? Do they even care about us as people? Or are we just numbers in a system? Is it only about helping the system make money? Looking back now, it was disgusting how they walked around from cell to cell, passing out psychiatric medications like water.

Much later when I told my psychiatrist back in Winnipeg that story, he was surprised because he hadn't heard of liquid Lithium and when he looked it up in the drug book he explained that it was hardly ever used, certainly not in Canada. When I asked my pharmacist about it, she agreed with my psychiatrist, and also said the Olanzapine wafer wasn't common here either. She thought perhaps that was how those medications were administered in the U.S. because both were easier to swallow, which would make life a lot easier for those who wanted to make sure the necessary medications were taken.

Good Will Hunting 2.0

My brain told me to continue working on my script. It had many different storylines and the characters could change their identities. There in Alameda, my mind was intermingled with a Hollywood triangle where life seemed perfect. While I created the script I lived the perfect bipolar fairytale lifestyle.

When the L.A. psychiatrist came to see me the next day, I was doing my script and yelling and mumbling to myself. I yelled, "Fucker! Fucker!" When I saw him approach the cell door I immediately stopped my script and went to speak to him.

He asked, "Did you take your medication last night?"

"No, they didn't give them to me." And then I again asked, "Can I have a bra?"

"Sorry, those undergarments are not given to inmates in jail."

"Well, can I have a vitamin?" I wanted him to know I had a nutrition degree. I went on to tell him that I took a nutrition class and that calcium and magnesium were important minerals to take, but if you took them together, they counteracted.

When he asked me if I would meet with my parents, I agreed, and then I asked, "Can they bring me vitamins?"

Right after the psychiatrist left, I started back at my script.

In my bipolar fairytale movie *Good Will Hunting 2.0*, there were three lead actors and me. While I was working on my script a jail worker brought me some food. It was gross—rice, beans, gravy, bread and a burrito—yuck!

The white tissue wrapper around the burrito had the name of a municipality located in Mexico called Los Cabos. I removed about thirty of the beans from the food and set them on the window ledge, allowing them to dry overnight. My brain told me I could figure out the title number for the new *Oceans* movie by counting the beans—fourteen . . . fifteen . . . twenty-four. I strategically lined up the perfect number of beans—twenty-six; perfect because eight was my favourite number and eight beans separated perfectly into two and six. I then decided the setting for my movie would be Los Cabos.

I grabbed three beans that weren't a part of the twenty-six to symbolize the three main actors in my movie. I placed them in toilet paper and stuffed them in the pocket of my blue pants. I didn't have a good feeling about the dirty, dingy cell I was in so my hands picked up the food tray and chucked it against the wall of the bottom bunk. I didn't worry about the mess of food on the bottom bunk because that night I slept on the top bunk.

The next morning, a guard came around and looked at the state of my cell. “What happened here?”

My shoulders just shrugged.

The guard said, “Don’t worry,” and later that day they moved me to another cell.

The three main actors in *Good Will Hunting 2.0* were The Hawk, The Lion and The Bear. They were friends and formed a triangle between them. When my character was in the script, there were four characters and that made a diamond shape. Everything balanced out. The secret code was the three bean triangle, like the three amigos.

When I changed my pants and tossed them outside the cell, I suddenly remembered the secret beans wrapped in toilet paper. “Wait! I forgot something in the pocket.”

The jail guard pulled out the wad of toilet paper and unwrapped it to reveal the beans. She gave me a weird look, but I didn’t care because my mind was focused on my script and my secret code.

My brain told me the secret code—the three beans—was of huge significance to my script. The Hawk always brought the action into every scene and he knew everything; he had a hawk eye. The Lion was sometimes tame, but he knew how to stir it up. The Bear occasionally hibernated, but when you got in his way, watch out! Nobody knew those three characters were connected. If you saw them out somewhere, you would never know they even knew each other. That is why their triangle was so secretive. But the games and tricks they played were so conniving you’d wish you knew how they pulled things off.

That script was my way to get out of everything. “That wasn’t me talking to you. I was just rehearsing my script.” “I wasn’t yelling Fucker! Fucker! I was doing my script.”

It provided a hidden place where I could go to escape the haunted jail system and where I never got into any trouble.

Since my brain told me I was undercover and trying to help out the law, I thought they had strategically placed me in the new cell. It had nothing to do with tossing food against the wall and everything to do with the jail system needing me in that exact cell. From there my eyes could see everything that was happening downstairs, even when it was dark. There was a glassed area with a computer. One guard ducked into that room, entered data on the computer, and then ducked out again. It was like there was a laser beam that would set off an alarm if she touched it. She ducked in and out several times. There were also three inmates who stood beside the glass area. They passed each other things in a line-up. My sick mind thought they packed cocaine into each other's jail attire and that there was some form of cocaine party going on in the back room beside the desk. There was a folded wheelchair sitting in front of the computer room that was used to electrocute inmates; it just had to be plugged in. They would think they were getting wheeled somewhere, but instead they were going to be shocked to death. My mind knew that could happen because of the woman who got injected and curled inward. My mind knew Alameda was where you went to die.

Toilet Paper Bikini

The next day in the cell, I grabbed two maxi pads and some toilet paper. Swiftly I wrapped the toilet paper around my body, imitating the lines of a Herve Leger dress, to make a beautiful white toilet paper bikini. I stuck the maxi pads underneath both breasts for extra support. My brain told me the world was watching and I wanted them to see the many bruises all over my arms and legs. People needed to see the abuse my body had gone through. I stood on the desk-like piece of furniture in the cell in my toilet paper bikini so the world would see the lashings my body had taken. There I stood, happy someone would see. I thought I showed the world, but nobody saw a thing. Besides, who inside that jail system would ever vouch for me?

CHAPTER 26

Bail Hell

Even as my aunt and uncle took care of my parents a lot, my dad took care of my uncle a little bit as well because he had forgotten his Lipitor in Arizona and had to share my dad's. Each of them shared something with each other—tears, despair, sadness, and even Lipitor. They also shared the responsibility of coming up with my bail money. Because the angelic psychiatrist had placed me on a 5150 hold, I was finally being transferred to a hospital, but bail needed to be posted before that could happen.

Initially the amount was set at $20,000, but when a different city prosecutor suggested it be increased to $50,000, the assistant to my crook of a lawyer didn't object. That lawyer then suggested a bail bondsman he knew, but if my parents had paid the money that way, the bondsman would have charged them a non-refundable ten per cent compensation fee of $5,000 for his services.

My uncle thought if he transferred the $50,000 to his credit card, he would be able to get a cash advance on his Visa. But by the time he found out that wouldn't work, the banks had already closed and it was too late for him to cancel the transaction.

So instead, my parents and my aunt and uncle had to scrape together the money little by little, from various banks and credit cards. They could only get an advance of $5,000 per credit card, so getting the bail money ended up being a tedious process. They had to visit three or four different banks, all of which closed early on Saturdays. So it was a race against the clock to get and pay the bail money by the end of business on Saturday January 15. It had to be done by then because if it was, there was a good chance that during the court hearing two days later, the judge would release me to a hospital. After three and a half hours and many transactions at many banks, they came up with $50,000 in U.S. funds.

My aunt put the money in her small tan fossil bag with a dark brown shoulder strap. They had to go to a seedy area of L.A. in order to post the bail for me; my mom said my aunt held on very tight to the bag. When they arrived, there were a lot of bail bondsmen waiting in limos for individuals who needed to post bail. My parents and aunt and uncle walked right past everybody and went into the building where the people who collected the bail money were waiting in wickets behind plexiglass.

When my aunt pulled out the $50,000 in cash to post my bail, the woman behind the glass was shocked. "What are you doing bringing cash here?"

No L.A. Again

My lawyer was nothing special. He drew up a letter that stated I would pay $750 USD for the damage to the police cruiser and that I would not go back to the U.S. again. When my uncle saw that letter, he rewrote it and emailed back the changes—I would *not* pay the $750 USD and I *could* return to the U.S. at any time. The lawyer took my uncle's rewritten letter and read it verbatim in court that Monday. The judge granted the requests. If it wasn't for my uncle, I'm not sure I could have handled the idea of never returning to L.A. again.

My heart still aches at what my parents and aunt and uncle had to do to save me from that dirty, creepy jail system. Their strength, endurance, and suffering helped me suffer less.

Something should be done about a jail system where, according to Hare & Rose (CNN, 2016), 25 percent of the inmates are mentally ill. That percentage makes the system the largest mental institution in the country. There is something spine-chillingly wrong about individuals who are mentally ill and not in their right mind being locked up in jail instead of being taken to hospital or a proper mental health facility.

If the psychiatric hospitals in L.A. don't have the space, why not close off some of the wings of the massive prisons and jails and turn *them* into hospitals, especially since the mentally ill are already taken there? Turn the cells into rooms with doors; hire doctors and nurses who are empathetic, compassionate, and qualified, and who understand mental illness; get rid of the blue and yellow attire that tag us as mentally ill; make a green space with a waterfall; incorporate mindfulness, yoga, and meditation; and treat the mentally ill with care, dignity, and respect instead of killing their confidence, humiliating and degrading them, cuffing and shackling them, and locking them up all in jail cells.

Magician

On Monday January 17, a jail worker escorted me down to the ground floor. I was still shackled, but I didn't know why; I figured it was either because they didn't like me or they didn't trust me. In any case, after I was put in yet another cell, I began to work extremely hard for more than half an hour to try and release my shackles by contorting my body in many different ways.

Despite all that time locked up behind bars in small rooms, my body was still flexible from my gymnastics days, and I was able to easily go from one movement to the next. If anyone saw me, it would have looked like I was break dancing. I threw one leg over the top of the other and then my body spun around on the floor as I tried to release my shackles. A few times I thought they were so close to breaking, but they never did. When that didn't work, I sat on the bench in the cell, crisscrossing my legs, one on top of the other until I finally wrapped my leg around my calf. *There has to be some way out of these. Perhaps a release somewhere?* My body worked and worked and worked to break those shackles. When I was finally exhausted, I went for a pee break to the toilette in the cell.

Soon after, a paramedic came to my cell. After opening the door, he asked me to step outside and lie down on the stretcher he had with him. He was so calm and kind that I decided to go with him. He took me down an eerie hallway of the jail where the lighting was dismal. When he placed a clear plastic bag underneath my legs filled with items I couldn't identify, my eyes filled with tears. My mind told me the bag had bones and carcasses in it and they were using my body's energy to help figure out the jail killing drama.

The paramedic then handed an African American guard in his twenties a piece of paper, and asked him to sign it. The guard refused.

"Why won't you sign her release form?"

With those words, my eyes filled with tears again and I began to sob uncontrollably. I cried so much and so hard, my insides ached. I had been through too much pain and trauma for one individual to handle.

The paramedic pointed to me with tears pouring down my face, and simply said, "See?"

The guard finally grabbed the pen and signed my release form.

I firmly believe if that paramedic had not stuck up for me in the jail that day, the guard may not have signed the release form and I might still have been trapped in that terrible jail system.

A Little Bit of Kindness

After being released from jail, the paramedic told me I was being transported by ambulance to the Los Angeles County + USC Medical Center (LAC+USC). He rode in the ambulance with me, and I felt very at ease with him. At one point, he asked me for my medical number, or whatever it is they have in the U.S., and when I couldn't tell him, he looked at my pinky-red bracelet. When I told him I was Canadian, he asked if I was married or single.

"Married."

"What is your name?"

"Sandra Bloom." My mind told me I had married Orlando Bloom sometime during the night I was at Van Nuys Police Station.

The paramedic looked at my bracelet again and asked, "How did that happen?"

I shrugged my shoulders.

He smiled and said, "Sometimes these things just happen."

Even when I said peculiar things, that paramedic didn't make me feel small, or tell me I was wrong, or say, no, that didn't happen. Because he was so kind to me, my eyes filled up with tears once again, not because I was depressed or at the beginning of a manic episode, but because I was letting go of all the pent-up emotions after days lost and locked in the L.A. County jail system.

The paramedic then pulled out his phone and showed me a picture of a car; even though the screen was cracked, I could still see the car clearly enough. He said he was going to paint it yellow and black. Those were the exact colours of my *Kill Bill* outfit when I competed in fitness competitions. My mind thought, *What a coincidence*, and I felt connected to him.

The paramedic smiled again and said, "When you get out, you should consider being a magician."

I think he told me that because he *had* seen me in the cell that day, contorting my body and working so hard to break the shackles. Shackles I never deserved to wear.

LAC+USC

When the paramedic took me into the waiting area at LAC+USC Medical Center, I didn't want him to leave.

"Can you stay with me?" I pleaded.

He stayed for quite a while, but then said he really had to go. That upset me terribly. He was the first person I felt safe with since I was arrested. Before he left, he handed me the clear plastic bag, and that's when I realized it was actually filled with all my belongings. He stayed until I was finally taken to the treatment area.

I was sitting on a chair up against the wall when a female doctor came to talk to me; it did not go well. For about half an hour we disagreed about taking out my contact lenses; I had worn them for ten days straight. I said I didn't want to give up my vision.

"It's my first night out of jail and I have no idea where I am or what is going on. Why would I want blurred vision on top of all of that?"

Yes, I was free and out of jail, but I was still lost. My mind had no concept of anything. *Life is so unfair.*

Eventually, I agreed to take out my contacts. My vision was blurred, but I just carried on.

Down the hall were a couple of patients locked in rooms, freaking out and yelling. The screams and ruckus they caused were not abnormal or scary. Those patients were just going through something and they needed a release. Imagine if your brain didn't work right, you had no control over its function, and some convoluted, scary image was going through your head. You'd scream, too.

At the end of that hallway were two rooms filled with stretchers. One room housed six patients, including me. When my neighbour on the next stretcher told me she had been abused, I walked over to the office in the corner so I could tell a doctor about it. The doctor in there was clearly very busy and simply replied, "I will get to it."

To my surprise and delight, it was the angelic psychiatrist who came to see me in jail and who placed me on a 5150 hold so I could be transferred to a hospital. We didn't speak a lot while I was there, but I was grateful he got me out of jail so I could get better and go home.

In another room were about eight stretchers of men lying along the wall. Just as I was about to step into the washroom, my eyes looked up to see a guy whacking off in there. For the rest of my hospitalization in L.A., I made sure my feet always had socks on whenever I was in the washroom.

When my parents arrived at LAC+USC, it was the first time we had seen each other in eleven days. Before that could happen, however, the angelic psychiatrist sat them down and talked with them to reassure them I was okay. After listening to their concerns, he said, "The California system is a bureaucratic mess." Then he explained that LAC+USC was a jail hospital, I would be there for one night while I was assessed, and then I would be transferred to a community hospital the next day.

That psychiatrist was the first person my parents met in L.A. who was kind and empathetic and didn't brush them off. He was truly a breath of fresh air in that stale system.

Martin Luther King Jr. Community Hospital

The next day I was taken to the Martin Luther King Jr. Community Hospital in East L.A. Jail had caused me so much trauma that I was stressed out and became terrified of my new roommate. She was an older lady in her fifties with dark hair, and we each had a twin bed. In my mind she was a cannibal and ate people for dinner. When she opened and closed her middle finger to her thumb, I thought it was a sign she was a killer and that she was waving goodbye to me because I was the next to be eaten.

My mind was terrified. Because my mind was ill, I wouldn't tell any of the medical staff my thoughts. I couldn't tell them I was afraid to go to the restroom in the hospital because I had to pass the cannibal's bed. I eventually had to go so bad that I ran to the toilet, but wouldn't sit down because I didn't want to touch what she had touched.

Eventually, I couldn't take it anymore, and I asked one of the nurses if I could please sleep in another room. To my surprise, he said yes and agreed to let me sleep in another room by myself for two nights.

After that, I took an afternoon nap in cannibal's room when she wasn't there. When I awoke suddenly from a dream, I was under the covers, my body was shaking, and I screamed. In my dream, cannibal had rolled down the hall in a wheelchair on the psychiatric ward I was in, but she was only a skeleton. No hair, no skin, only bones. I thought that because she was so hungry, she had eaten her own flesh. Then I thought she had also eaten three hundred and seventeen people and that I was next.

Never in my life had I been so extremely frightened. A few days later, cannibal stopped by my bed and started waving again. I was afraid what that meant until she explained, "I'm saying my prayers."

A lightning bolt instantly woke me up from that nightmare. She was no cannibal, just an older lady saying her prayers. Because of what happened at LAC+USC, I began to wear socks on my feet while I was in the shower. When my nurse Dwayne asked why, my shoulders just shrugged. I couldn't tell him about the guy who whacked off in the other hospital. He may have wondered if there was something wrong in my thought process, but in actuality, the reason was quite legitimate. One afternoon Dwayne tucked a couple of extra pairs of socks in the drawer of the nightstand of my drab, neutral hospital room. He wanted to make sure I never ran out of socks.

Dwayne always sat outside the door of the shower—standard procedure to make sure patients didn't harm themselves. There was no danger of me harming myself; I was more interested in singing because singing was therapeutic and soothed my soul. Every day in the hospital, I sang songs as an internal treatment to heal and soothe myself, and every day Dwayne told me my singing was very good. During the time I was at Martin Luther, I was taking Lithium, a mood stabilizer, and Olanzapine, an antipsychotic. In an undated letter to my lawyer, the doctor said I was improving as a result of the medication, but I didn't notice them helping at all. It actually took a long period of time—at least six weeks—and a couple of changes in medication before the meds started to help and my mind became clearer. That's when I began to realize everything in my bipolar fairytale movie was false, and then one day I switched out of it completely. The light went out and the movie was gone.

One Thousand and Eight Hundred Miles

Although the Community Hospital was in a rougher part of L.A., it was fifty miles from the hotel where my parents and aunt and uncle were staying in Burbank.

"Thank goodness for GPS," declared my uncle, who had already put 1,800 miles on his car in L.A. driving between the different jails, hospitals, and banks.

That entire experience totalled twenty days—ten days in jail, one night in a hospital jail ward, and ten days in the community hospital. For too many of those days I was lost in the system, and neither my parents nor my aunt and uncle could find me.

One night the four of them were too exhausted to drive back to Burbank, so they stayed in La Quinta Hotel close to the hospital. They all shared a room. My parents were so distraught over everything that they couldn't handle staying alone.

I'm not sure even now that I can fully appreciate the stress they all felt and the pressure they were under during that entire time in L.A. What I do appreciate is that while a bunch of frantic things were happening to my parents and my aunt and uncle behind the scenes, they never gave up on me, even when I was lost, even when I said I didn't want to see them. They did everything they could to get me released.

When I was admitted to the hospital, they visited me every day. Unfortunately, none of the other patients had any visitors, but I did and that made me very happy. Sometimes I made fun of my uncle, stomping across the floor like he did and saying what he would say to my aunt. He was usually the jokester and always bugged other people, so I decided to bug him. My sense of humour was coming out. Mom brushed my hair every day to soothe me. It meant everything to me to finally be with my family.

My psychiatrist from Winnipeg was in constant contact with my parents. He wasn't only interested in how I was doing, but also wanted to see how they were doing; he did what he could to calm their fears and soothe their souls. There are no words to describe how grateful my family was toward my psychiatrist, and there are absolutely no words even now to describe what it means to me that my parents and aunt and uncle were there for me and found a way to help me. If it wasn't for them, I would have been shuffled around and lost even more in the Los Angeles County jail system.

Leaving on a Jet Plane

The sun shone brilliantly in a clear sky on my last day in L.A. As I stood in the open courtyard right in the centre of the Martin Luther King Jr. Community Hospital, surrounded by basketball nets and green potted plants, my eyes were innocent, my lips were chapped, my long, blonde hair hung on my shoulders, and my legs were firmly planted. I wore no makeup, but I was wearing hospital pyjamas. My hand was holding a piece of paper Dwayne had given me with the lyrics of the song I used to sing over and over in the shower.

As I stood there, my hands shook because I was so nervous. The staff had suggested that before I leave, I sing for all the doctors, patients, and nurses, and especially my parents. When my mouth opened, my voice began to sing "Leaving on a Jet Plane."

The only person missing that day was my beloved brother Michael. He had introduced me to Chantal Kreviazuk's version of that song after the album *Armageddon* was released. Chantal is from Winnipeg and her family suffers from mental illness—a remarkable coincidence that a singer from Winnipeg's song soothed my soul so much while I was suffering with mental illness.

So there I was in broad daylight belting out the lyrics to the best of my ability; I remember thinking at one point the echo was better in the shower. My voice cracked a couple of times, but I made it through the song and everyone applauded.

Right after I sang that song, I boarded a "jet plane" and left Los Angeles. It was a small medical plane— a leer jet, in fact—with only enough room for my parents, two paramedics, the pilot and co-pilot, and me. My parents sat behind me, while the paramedics sat facing me and to my left. There was no washroom, but there was a stretcher in the aisle. I knew I wouldn't be needing that.

Before going back to Arizona to continue their interrupted vacation, my aunt and uncle decided to spend one more night in L.A. They stayed in the same apartment I had rented in Burbank where they and my parents worked so hard to secure both my release from jail and my return home to get the help I needed.

When we landed in Winnipeg, the paramedic asked, "Do you want to keep your L.A. County yellow top and blue pants?" I not so politely declined.

Who in their right mind would want to keep that loud, conspicuous, demeaning jail attire that screamed to the world I have a chemical imbalance in my brain? No thanks. I'd had enough of people treating me like a second class citizen in jail because of that gaudy yellow and blue coloured clothing. I am a person and should not be defined by my illness.

I was about to enter my fourth hospitalization—fifth, if you counted the post-jail community hospital stop. When the plane landed in Winnipeg, my bed at the Health Sciences Centre was ready. The paramedics told my parents they had never seen anyone walk right into a ward like I did. I stayed there for seven weeks.

When You Add it All Up

On top of the $50,000 my family had to pay for my bail, there were other costs that would have ruined them if I hadn't purchased insurance—a mere $228 for three months—before my journey to L.A. Ironically, nobody knew whether or not I even had insurance, so I was sent to the Martin Luther King Jr. Community Hospital because that's where they send people who can't afford insurance.

For the ten days I was there, my bills totalled approximately an astronomical $46,000, all of which was automatically covered by insurance. It also cost another $22,000 for an air ambulance to take me home. And there was the cost to get my Sunfire out of lock up and ship it back to Winnipeg.

My parents fought every day with the insurance company until they eventually agreed to reimburse *all* those expenses. The insurance company then wrote me a letter saying I couldn't take out emergency medical insurance with them again.

It was shortly after I got back that I gave my dad power of attorney over me so he would be able to help immediately if anything like that every happened again.

When my uncle got home to Canada, he went online to file a complaint with Internal Affairs about my poor treatment in the system. He followed the manual for protocol to the letter. One of the first mistakes the LAPD made was that when I was booked, they should have arranged immediately for a doctor to give me a proper mental health check-up. My uncle listed all the places where protocol had been breached. He spoke to investigators in the system. He spent countless hours going through the process of fighting for me, but in the end it all came to naught.

The complaint was eventually dropped because the stress of the entire experience, the failings of the jail system, and the burden of fighting for what was right was altogether too much for my family to handle. Besides, who in the system would vouch for me? They would all just stick up for each other.

It should be much easier to lodge a complaint. It was bad enough for me, who had a family who loved me, cared for me, and supported me through the ordeal, and *still* the complaint process was arduous. Imagine somebody who was mentally ill with *no* support trying to lodge a complaint about that awful jail system, a system obviously set up to make it almost impossible to lodge any kind of complaint.

CHAPTER 27

God

Every day in February and March 2011, I reached for the receiver of the phone hanging on the wall in the psychiatric hospital ward to call my friend George. He managed the Boston Pizza restaurant the first time I worked there. He was also the only friend I talked to while I was hospitalized. I didn't contact Emma or Maggie or anyone else because I didn't want them to know I was in the hospital.

The only reason I called George was because I needed an outlet, someone to talk to, someone who would make me laugh and help me escape my surroundings. Although I didn't tell George I was actually *in* the hospital, I got the distinct impression that he had figured it out, but later on, that proved not to be the case.

One day while I was eating lunch, some of the other patients were annoying me with their antics. I stood up from my tray of food, pushed back my chair, and announced in a loud voice, "I'm going to call God." I knew it would get to them.

A patient in her fifties exclaimed, "Oh no, oh no, she's going to call God. Somebody help me."

I immediately walked to the phone booth, followed by gasps from the lunch room. As my hand clenched the receiver I spoke into the mouthpiece.

"How do you get someone to change?"

George answered, "Sometimes you can't *get* people to change."

That was interesting, and different to what Paul had said when I asked him the same question a few years before.

I went to take a bath, one of two I usually had every day to soothe myself.

After almost two weeks I was allowed out of my hospital pajamas and into street clothes. It was the staff's way of saying I was getting better. I was thrilled beyond belief, finally free of the neutral, characterless hospital pyjamas. It also made me feel more independent because I no longer looked like all the other patients.

I called my mom many times a day. She listened to me, talked to me, and patiently answered any questions I had. When they came to visit, Dad would always look right at me and say, "Today is a good day. I'm going to get better." And then he would make me repeat that back to him. Once, he even wrote it out for me on a pad of paper in my room so I would remember to keep repeating it even after they had left. One day he brought me a picture and placed it on the desk beside my bed. It showed a stork trying to swallow a frog, but the frog was choking the bird so that it wouldn't be eaten. At the bottom it said, "Don't Ever Give Up."

That photo used to hang on the wall in his office. It meant so much to me that he would share it with me when I needed it most.

I am so blessed to have my parents. They visited me and supported me every day I was at Health Sciences. I truly believe they are the reason I always found a way through my illness and recovered so well.

"What the Hell is a Gluck?"

One day while sitting on the ugly green-blue hospital furniture in the television room, I told Fred, a patient in his fifties with scruffy black hair and a moustache, my story about the barber shop scene in L.A. Fred was hospitalized because he tried to commit suicide. I told him the part in the story where I said, “I’ve got a Gluck and I’m going to blow this bitch down.”

He started laughing hysterically. “You said a Gluck. What the hell is a Gluck? I was a police officer for twenty-five years. I never heard of a Gluck. I had a *Glock*. Is that what you mean?”

I was stunned. “It’s called a Glock?”

He laughed again. “Yes.”

And in that moment I realized I had been using my dad’s word—a dadism. My mind flashed back to the barbershop garage. *No wonder I didn’t really scare anyone.*

Even my fake undercover get-up was a joke.

After seven weeks I was finally discharged and sent home on Lithium and Clozapine. I remained on both medications for only six months because they sedated me too much and made me very drowsy. As well, the Clozapine had lowered my neutrophil count—a type of white blood cell that plays a major role in fighting infection—into the cautionary zone, which meant it would be more difficult for my body if I got any kind of infection. Abilify was then tried and discontinued because of akathisia, which made me feel restlessness and unable to stay still. Olanzapine was substituted then discontinued because of fatigue and a painful glaze. Later I was prescribed Ziprasidone, but could only tolerate a small dosage because the higher dosage caused restless legs syndrome. Finding the right combination of psychiatric medications was frustrating, but I agreed with my psychiatrist that I needed to stay on them because of the jail situation. I knew I could never go there again.

Being ill and in hospital takes such a toll on my mind, my body, and my life that I always need to spend time resting after I am released. But with all the trauma of being in jail and in L.A. and then another seven weeks at Health Sciences, I particularly needed time to recover. I moved back to my parents' home where I worked my way toward being well.

During that time, I was also looking for some kind of job. Even though I was tired, had no energy, and needed to recover from my ordeal, I wanted to work, I wanted to support myself, to be independent. But I knew it could sometimes take six months of recovery before finding gainful employment, so I started sending out a number of applications as soon as I possibly could.

After my hospitalization, Emma and Maggie came to my parents' house for coffee, or we went for a walk and talked. Sometimes they brought their kids, and sometimes not. We also met at Kildonan Park and went for a leisurely stroll. Maggie even picked me up and took me to her daughter's soccer practice, and we used the opportunity to catch up. Occasionally, Larissa and Tatiana also came over to the house to see me and visit.

Four months after my hospitalization, I finally got a job. It wasn't the one I wanted—my old Territory Manager job—and was well below my qualifications, as was the wage, but I was determined to work and to do whatever was necessary to hold down a job, so I sucked it up and went to work. I was a Retail

Service Specialist (Team Lead) for a grocery store whose head office was in Winnipeg. I travelled to grocery stores doing produce audits, out of stock audits, and price checks.

Up until that point in my life, I often thought I was defined by my education or career, but taking the Retail Service Specialist position taught me that life is about tiny stepping stones instead of one giant leap. You can't always get what you want right away, but you can set a goal and work toward it. Working helps with mental illness because it gets you out of the house, helps you socialize, allows you to use your mind, and gives you a purpose—"A reason to get up in the morning," as my psychiatrist in Winnipeg always said.

An Ugly Memory Makes a Wonderful Scene

While I worked, I continued to pursue my passion, signing up for three different classes at Prairie Theatre Exchange—Acting on Camera (twenty weeks, starting October 2011), Advanced Acting on Camera (ten weeks, starting January 2012), and another Advanced Acting on Camera (seven weeks, starting April 2012).

The acting classes were held in downtown Winnipeg on the third floor of Portage Place Mall. I always sang while driving to class, and why not. I was in my happy place because I was on my way to doing something I loved. I made sure to practise and memorize my lines at home beforehand so I would be ready to perform.

One night in late March, I was performing a scene for the group. It was one of my last scenes in that class because the session was almost over. My acting instructor, Ed, was tall, had a brown goatee, and usually wore a t-shirt. He looked at me and told me, "In your first take, you were experiencing anger. Anger is usually a cover for another emotion. So this time, aim more toward a sadder take, and see where that takes you."

During the second take I thought of that guard who stood at my cell and told me to show myself to him. That moment always stops me, pains me, and fills me with sadness. When I think about what he did to me, I weep and feel exposed, hurt, needy, and vulnerable. It was an ugly memory that made for a wonderful scene.

After the performance, there was only silence. My fellow actors were intrigued, and I felt they were right there with me. It was a brilliant moment that made me feel great, but also like I wanted to cry.

Ed asked, "What was the difference between the two takes?"

I could only tell him, "I was thinking about pain in my life." I couldn't explain anything more because that pain was carried in a hidden place I only shared with myself. There was nothing that could be done about that day in the courthouse jail, but I had taken away some of its power over me by using it to better myself as an actor.

The scene struck so deep that Ed could tell I was in pain. I had never seen him give anyone a hug but he asked me, "Do you need a hug?"

Yes, I do.

Funny how most of my acting teachers always knew how I felt without me ever having to say a word.

"What is the Cause of Your Illness?"

One summer night in June 2012, George and I went for a scenic drive. Because he had phoned my parents every day I was in the hospital, we all thought he knew why I was there, so I decided to try and explain my illness to him.

"You know how I was mentally ill?"

He blabbered, "Uh . . . I . . . uh . . . no."

Then why did you call my mom every day to ask if I was okay?

And then it hit me. He had supported me so much while I was ill not because he knew everything I was going through, but because he was my friend and just wanted to be there for me. I felt safe sharing my story with him, but I was wrong.

I told him I have bipolar and what that meant, what happens to me when I am in a manic state, and why I was in the hospital.

"Are you sick right now?" he asked.

"No, I'm not sick."

"Well, what is the cause of your illness?"

"I don't know the cause, George. I only know that sometimes my brain doesn't function right."

"What does your doctor think?"

"My doctor thinks I'm fine."

"What do your parents think?"

"I'm not ill right now."

Then for some reason, I told him about Los Angeles and that night in Burbank.

He simply said, "You were really far gone."

There wasn't a shred of empathy in his voice.

Things changed for us after that, and even though I continued to talk to him for a while, we were never again as close as we had been. In the end, George turned out to be unsympathetic, which caused me a lot of pain in my life. That showed me that sometimes even close friends don't really understand mental illness.

Accepting Your Limitations is Part of Growing Up

A few days later, I went to see my psychiatrist in Winnipeg. I had developed a good relationship with him during our many sessions over the years. He had helped me through so much and helped my parents as well, particularly during the time I was in L.A. He always listened to me talk about my issues, my anxieties, my hopes, and my dreams.

That day, he listened as I talked for almost thirty minutes about George and his lack of empathy toward me. He listened as I explained how the pain still lingered in my heart from my experiences in L.A. He listened as I itemized my acting journey—my attempt to pursue acting at least five times in three different cities, including L.A., where two of the three times I was there, my illness had sent me home within three weeks of my arrival. He listened when I said, "I still want to pursue acting in L.A."

I guess he listened to my acting downfall stories one too many times because then, with a single sentence, he shattered my dreams by shooting an arrow deep into my heart.

"Accepting your limitations is part of growing up."

That was a painful moment for me because I knew he was actually telling me to give up on the idea of pursuing acting as a career.

It didn't help when he used himself as an example by saying he would never be a pianist or an NBA basketball player. The damage was already done; he had made me feel like a child. My one passion, my one dream in life, diminished by just a few words, shot down by the one person who had helped me through some of the most difficult struggles in my life.

What hurt the most was that he came across as scientific and clinical, only seeing me in black and white. But I was grey, a creative soul desperately looking for a way to express my true self. Unfortunately, my psychiatrist had only succeeded in casting a shadow over my soul.

By the time I left his office, my painful feelings hadn't dissipated. I knew my heart had to find a way to pick up and carry on, despite being wounded by that particular arrow. I'm not sure how I managed it, but for the first time ever, I didn't cry in his office. He had done so much for my family and me and I didn't feel like I could show him that his words had broken my heart. I did, however, cry all the way home.

When I think now about what happened then, I understand that my psychiatrist's goal was to help me live a balanced and stable life. He could see that my pursuit of acting had only managed to push me further and further away. And he was trying to tell me that an acting career was a shot in the dark, an unstable option, the continued pursuit of which could lead to a mentally unbalanced life. I know now my psychiatrist was only looking out for my best interests.

It was the acceptance of the real meaning of that session with him that allowed me to move forward. And I needed to move forward to survive. My passion was still acting—and would always *be* acting—but it was time for me to look the other way.

You Probably Wouldn't Want to Marry Someone like Me

Because my illness would sometimes creep up on me, it was always in the back of my mind. In February 2013, I started a new job in a call centre, selling high-end hotels to people from all over the world. It was like being a travel agent, finding out what people were specifically looking for, and selling them on a particular hotel that met their needs. Although I was based in Winnipeg, I was recommending hotels in New York, Los Angeles, Miami, and Chicago.

I trained for seven weeks, but only worked in the job for two. I simply couldn't do it. Anxiety overwhelmed me, and my psychiatrist gave me the anti-anxiety medication Diazepam to make it go away. That didn't help, and my brain ended up working overtime. I suspected the anxiety was the result of my time in the L.A. jail because I never had it in my life before then. When I finally quit, I was so upset because I really wanted to be successful in that job.

In 2013 I went to Las Vegas for the wedding of someone I knew in Calgary. My good friend Collin, who I had met back in 2005 and reconnected with in 2012, decided to tag along as my guest. Collin didn't know my whole story, but I did tell him I'd had a hard life and that, as a result, my doctor said I had a bit of depression and anxiety. Then I explained that because of the anxiety, I didn't think I'd be able to go because it was so debilitating that we should cancel. He fixed the problem by not buying *any* insurance when he booked our trip, and he reassured me by saying, "It might be good for you to get away."

He was right. It felt good to be somewhere else for a while. It also felt good when Collin, who had been having a hard time with some of his friends, told me, "Sometimes people like you for your downfalls. I mean, look at you and all of your friends. Nobody has ever left you." That made me smile. He also gave me guy advice when I asked for it, and showed me how to use humour when talking to guys and to put out the same language they did. We hung out, ate Thai food, and watched a reality television series called *The Hills*.

The wedding reception was at a restaurant in the Wynn Hotel. At one point, I had to leave the reception because my sparkling Guess high-heeled shoes that I had bought at Ross Dress for Less in L.A. were hurting me. The part of the shoe where the toes peeked out was digging into my big toe and made it bleed. Collin came with me to make sure I got to my room and back without any problem. I walked as far as I could through the hotel with my shoes on, but eventually had to take them off.

Almost immediately, a security guard came over and told me I couldn't walk through the hotel without wearing shoes. Because of my time in jail, I was still very afraid of anyone in law enforcement. I got highly emotional and almost cried. I explained to Collin, "I'm upset because of my past. If you could only understand."

He didn't need to know my story; instead he simply offered to buy me new shoes. I declined because I knew they would be too expensive. Then out of nowhere a lady asked me if I wanted to borrow her sandals. She saw I was upset and overheard that I couldn't walk in my shoes or my bare feet. I thanked her, borrowed her sandals, and went to my room to get another pair of shoes. Luckily, on the way back to the reception I did find the lady who lent me her sandals and gave them back.

Before long, we were back at the reception and later on went to a club. It was my first time out socially in a large group since my time in jail. A friend of the groom asked me to marry him. We had never met before, but there was a compelling energy between us. He was not my usual type. He asked me several times that night, so I knew he was serious about getting married. He made me feel beautiful because he was instantly attracted to me and knew what he wanted.

After the vacation he asked to see me again. He came to Winnipeg on business and we went out to dinner. Later that night when he talked about marriage again, I said, "You probably wouldn't want to marry someone like me."

His response was gut wrenching. "Do you have a little bit of crazy going on?"

That hurt me so much that I talked about it in session soon after. My psychiatrist wasn't too fond of what that fellow had said, and he made a funny joke about what my response to him should have been.

CHAPTER 28

Cookie Sales in Calgary

The L.A. County jail system was the wrong place to send me. It did nothing to help me and did not look out for my best interests. Instead, it caused trauma in my life that gave me anxiety and often made it very difficult to cope. I had never suffered with anxiety before, and it added to the challenges of finding permanent full-time employment. That was already difficult enough given all the time off from illness in my life. While I looked for employment, I worked on a casual basis doing nutritional jobs at a bakery, but I knew I wanted something more, something that would allow me to show what I was capable of doing.

When everything seemed like it would never get better, I decided to send my resume to my old consumer packaged goods company in Alberta. In the days that followed, there were phone interviews, I flew to Calgary (on my own dime) for more interviews, and got my old cookie sales job back in the grocery industry. It was July 2013, two and a half years after my jail experience.

My psychiatrist told me I was ready to go. I told him if I couldn't be an actress, Territory Manager was the position I wanted. During my last session with him before I left

Winnipeg I explained that he was one of my best friends; he said the feeling was mutual. Even when he wasn't around I wanted to call him to tell him about my life. To me, that was the epitome of a good, kind, and empathetic psychiatrist. He was invaluable, and my heart and my mind wished that he could have been in my back pocket whenever I needed him. He wished me well and told me that I had a community to come home to if I needed it.

After saying goodbye to my friends, I flew out to Calgary with my suitcase and backpack filled with clothes, shoes, and toiletries. I was definitely ready to start work. My Aunt Laura and Uncle Doug, who had helped my parents rescue me from jail, graciously allowed me to stay with them while I searched for a place to live. Six weeks later I moved into a condo and started to build a new life for myself.

My job was going well—I was good at sales—but all I could handle in those early days was work and sleep. The pills I used to get to sleep took quite a toll on my body, but I was afraid if I didn't sleep, I would get ill again. Down in L.A., no sleep was what triggered my bipolar and led me to jail, and I knew I never wanted to go back to that dingy jail cell again. For me, sleep is the number one priority for my life and staying well.

A Vicious Cycle

Despite how his words had hurt me, I continued to email and talk with the guy I met at the destination wedding. We even visited each other three times; it was easier then because I lived in Calgary and he lived in Nelson, British Columbia.

However, after his last visit in October 2013, he didn't call me. Ten days passed without a word, and even though I essentially knew then the relationship, such that it was, had ended, it made me question my illness. *Does he think I* do *have a little bit of crazy going on?* Nobody can tell I have bipolar. They only know about the illness if I tell them. That guy not calling me played with my mind, raised questions, and shook my self-esteem. He had recently lost his job and had gone travelling to some tropical location. When he finally contacted me, it was because he had a layover in Calgary and wanted to crash at my place. I told him he wasn't staying with me.

We messaged the odd time after that, but around Christmas 2013, he hurt me all over again and made my heart ache. It wasn't because we wouldn't even be friends anymore, but because he cited reasons I couldn't do anything about. When he said "the distance between us" and "I've been hurt so bad I will not let it happen again," I thought those excuses were weak, an easy way out, intended to let him off the hook. I blamed myself and the illness for him not talking to me or wanting to continue as friends.

Ever since my time in jail, I was scared of having a relationship because it would mean I'd have to open up to someone and tell them my story, and I wasn't ready to do that. Everything that guy did and said played with my mind, and made me angry and scared to the point that I decided not to pursue another relationship. *What would stop the next individual I meet from leaving and not being willing or able to give me a valid reason why?* Being alone was less painful, less emotional, and a lot simpler. It was easier not to have to explain my life and then be left in the dust questioning my illness.

No matter how much I wanted to, letting go of the memories about that incident in the jail cell with the guard was extremely difficult. The suffering my mind, heart, and body endured was stressful and a complete and continuing shock to my system. The pain lingered and pushed right into my soul. Talking to people about the jail itself was one thing, but having all the haunting memories flash back in my mind was traumatic and left me feeling miserable. Learning to let go of that agonizing pain caused me to stop loving myself. I stopped loving my good qualities, stopped loving my inside beauty, stopped loving my outside beauty, and stopped believing that I deserved the very best.

I have haunting memories of when I was in jail in L.A., like being stripped and hurt by five guards who called me princess. Afterward, when an associate in one of the big box stores where I work called me a princess just because I dressed up, my mind went immediately to that jail experience. Any princess items I see, such as a princess Halloween costume, stickers, or a doll, immediately make me think of jail and the pain my body endured.

Whenever I see the scar under my chin, I remember the guard who bashed my face into the concrete. That particular flashback comes complete with blood trickling down my face. Whenever my mind flashes back to the time I exposed myself to one of the guards, my heart aches and I cover myself to hide my shame.

I didn't want to constantly relive my dusty past, and I did want to find a way back to loving myself. In the fall of 2013 I found myself a general practitioner. I also started playing soccer again. I wanted to get more exercise and try to meet people in Calgary. Even though I was only playing once a week, it was difficult because the games were late at night, I didn't really meet anyone, and I got very tired. When I added in work and sleep, it was a vicious cycle. I was afraid of getting ill again and knew if I didn't sleep I *would* get ill, so sleeping pills were my only option. I popped one every night, and yet three months into the job, my anxiety got the better of me. It debilitated me and took over my mind.

Getting the Help I Needed

When I initially moved to Calgary, I asked my psychiatrist in Winnipeg if he knew anyone there he could recommend for me. Unfortunately he didn't, but he was able to get me a phone number I could call to self-refer to a psychiatrist. When I called that number, I was told I had to wait at least six weeks for an appointment. In the meantime, I had appointments with my G.P. My psychiatrist in Winnipeg emailed me my medical summary so I could print it off and give it to the G.P. while I waited to see a psychiatrist.

Having a G.P. was at least something, but I was largely without other help if I needed it. Because everything in Calgary was closed at night, except for emergency, there were essentially no other medical outlets available to me. That was particularly frustrating, especially since I used to be able to call my psychiatrist in Winnipeg at any hour of the day or night.

That G.P. has become an integral part of my care. He arranges counselling sessions with me and often bridges the gap if I need someone to talk to. He also prescribes medication to treat my thyroid problems that are the result of taking Lithium. What's interesting is that in Calgary, it takes three people—a G.P., psychiatrist, and therapist—to do what in Winnipeg was done by only one person.

You're Complicated

One night in October, I wasn't feeling well. I had major anxiety after working all day in sales. I really only knew two other people in Calgary, besides my aunt and uncle, and one of those was Melanie, my friend from high school; I was friends with her and her twin sister Larissa. Melanie was now a nurse, so I called her and asked if there was a doctor I could see at the clinic where she worked. She helped get me an appointment, and my aunt and uncle said they would go with me for support.

While I waited for that appointment, I moved back in with my aunt and uncle for a few days. There was no way I could be alone, and they wanted to help as much as they could.

The doctor was in her fifties. She listened as I told her about my meds and my anxiety, but she wouldn't do anything to help me. Instead, she said, "You're complicated."

Those words took a harpoon and stabbed me in the heart. She upset me and made me feel dreadful about myself.

When Melanie found out what had happened, she felt so bad, but I reassured her it wasn't her fault. On the plus side, Melanie and I have stayed in contact ever since.

Shaken up by that doctor and what she said only helped worsen my anxiety, so I called my psychiatrist in Winnipeg. He immediately set up a Skype session to help me. My first thought when we Skyped was, *He's not wearing his glasses;*

he's wearing contacts. During the session, my psychiatrist said I wasn't complicated, but I was complex. He listened to my anxieties and helped get me through the situation. *My knight in shining armour, always picking me up when I fall.*

Even though my psychiatrist lived far away, he helped me enough that I was able to get up every morning when my alarm rang and push myself to go to work. My wardrobe consisted of pants and jackets and clothes that covered my body and soul; they were protecting me from the memory of how I exposed myself in that jail cell. It was definitely a struggle, and every day at work I pushed myself as hard as I could.

New Psychiatrist and Therapist

In November, after waiting a little more than six weeks to get an appointment, I finally met my new psychiatrist, as well as a nurse therapist; they worked together and also apart.

The first time I met my psychiatrist, we didn't see eye to eye. He asked how much Ziprasidone I was on.

"Twenty milligrams."

He let his glasses slide down to the tip of his nose and looked at me over the top of his frames.

"That's not even a full dosage. A full dose is 80 mg."

That told me right away he hadn't even taken the time to look at my history of medications or my inability to tolerate some of them. That he wanted to put me on a stronger dosage of a medication I had to *stop* taking because of the side effects also told me he didn't understand what I had been through. And when he said, "Every medication is going to have a side effect; it's all in the way you handle it," that totally pissed me off.

I can't handle most *of the side effects these medications have.*

It was confusing and extremely frustrating to have a psychiatrist who didn't know how the various medications I had been on affected me.

You're not someone who cares about me; you're just a pill pusher. Another person who lacks the empathy to really help me. The first time I had my appointment with my therapist, Darrell looked me in the eyes and said, "I'm going to let you know if you are slipping."

What? Okay. I guess that's just your way of saying you are *looking out for me* and *my best interests.*

Even though Darrell was always supportive of whatever I needed to discuss, sessions with him were hard for me to grasp because I was used to the psychiatrist—*my* psychiatrist—being the one doing the therapy.

Anxiety

Near the end of 2013, lay-offs at work affected me tremendously and caused me to worry that I would be the next to go. It was fuel for the fire that drove my anxiety through the roof. By early January, my anxiety had worsened to the point that it was crippling. I felt it in my legs and just wanted to curl up into a ball and hide. My anxiety was so awful that in January 2014 Dad flew to Calgary and moved in with me. Unfortunately, Mom couldn't come as well because she had a frozen shoulder.

My anxiety was mind-numbing and painfully awful. Dad used my aunt and uncle's car to drive me around for work; he also helped around the condo and often cooked dinner or breakfast for me because I had no appetite and difficulty eating. His unconditional compassion was the only reason I survived that month. I worked and did nothing else besides come home, take an anti-anxiety pill, take a sleeping pill, and go to sleep. I had no quality of life, and because of my early-to-bed routine, there was no time to play soccer or socialize with friends. I was scared that if I went out I'd get anxiety and wouldn't be able to move or get back home. So I only existed at work and at my condo, and that was all.

Despite her pain, my mom helped me every day by talking with me over the phone. She is a voice of reason and my best friend.

As if my situation wasn't difficult enough for my parents, near the end of January, Mom was diagnosed with breast cancer. Dad immediately returned to Winnipeg to support her.

The news about Mom broke my heart. My parents were there through all my illnesses, but when Mom needed my support, I was too broken and too debilitated by anxiety to be there for her. Worrying about her and wishing I could help added to the weight of my anxiety. With everything going on and being as broken as I was, I barely managed to work another three months. Then during one particular session, my psychiatrist in Calgary looked me in the eyes and simply said, "Sometimes people need to take time off."

Was That You Who Went On a Rampage?

I was at my worst in April 2014 when George took things too far. Right after someone in Calgary killed five people at a house party, he texted me, "Was that you who went on a rampage and killed those people at the house party in Calgary, or was it someone else?" His attempt at sick humour was not at all funny. In fact, it crossed the mental health threshold. He knew about my mental health sufferings, and he should not have gone down that road. I can't say if his "joke" pushed me over the edge, but it definitely rubbed salt in the wound and made my anxiety even worse.

People often go down the wrong road with individuals who suffer from mental illness. They blame the individual, not the illness. But mental health issues are never the fault of the individual. And while it's true that sometimes those who have a mental illness are mean, violent, or insulting, they don't do any of that deliberately. In fact, often they are embarrassed afterward and feel regret.

If I could, I would tell those people not to be scared of an individual with mental illness just because they *have* a mental illness. Their brains don't function properly when they're ill, and it's not their fault. Yes, sometimes there are incidents where there is reason to be concerned or even afraid, but that happens much less that you might think. So instead, try to put yourself in their shoes for a moment. Imagine your brain has a completely different story going on, outside of reality. Imagine you are in a magic land where everything you wish for is coming true, pieces of your story are unfolding magically right in front of you, and everything is working itself out. While that magic land exists in your mind, you still have to deal with what is actually going on around you. And when the magic comes crashing down—in the end, the magic *always* comes crashing down—your life turns into a nightmare with pills and their side effects, the aftermath and the stigma. That is what it's like for us. So, don't judge a book by its cover, don't blame the individual with mental illness, and don't be afraid of us. We are people, too, and unless I told you, you wouldn't know I have bipolar, even if you met me.

Erratic Behaviour, Correctional Facility, and Quitting My Job

By May, I was a wreck. Mom was undergoing intensive radiation treatments—sixteen in all, Monday to Friday—and dealing with the side effects, and I wasn't functioning all that well because my anxiety was eating me alive. I knew I had to take some time off work and decided to go back to Winnipeg for a while.

I needed to take medical leave and asked my G.P. to fill out the necessary short-term disability forms. Because the forms said to "attach all relative forms," he attached the medical summary previously sent from my psychiatrist in Winnipeg. That included the statement "erratic behaviour in L.A. in early January 2011, involving vandalism of a police vehicle, led to incarceration initially in a correctional facility." Even though there were no outstanding charges against me from my time in L.A., there was no way those words could be sent to Human Resources and stored in the company file. I simply couldn't allow the people in the workplace to know about my mental illness or the fact that I went to jail. I was embarrassed and ashamed. *I would rather quit my job than send in that paperwork.*

Instead of applying for medical leave, I took two weeks of sick leave. I cleaned out my work vehicle and parked it at my aunt and uncle's place for my boss to pick up. I packed mostly shoes and clothes into my suitcase and backpack, and also took my work computer—which was returned to my aunt and uncle by Purolator a few days later so they could give it back to my boss. Then I flew to Winnipeg and moved in with my parents so I could get the medical attention I needed from my original psychiatrist.

Luckily, he was able to talk me down off the proverbial ledge. From the time I left work, I only had two weeks to decide whether to keep my job or let it go. My psychiatrist and I had four sessions where we discussed the disability forms and me quitting my job. He worked hard to convince me to keep my job and apply instead for short-term disability. I eventually spoke to someone in Human Resources and sent them the application, complete with my psychiatric history. Although I knew it would be confidential and no one else at work would find out, sending in that form was one of the toughest, most anxiety-provoking decisions of my life.

With my psychiatrist's encouragement, I asked for and was given a short-term leave. During that time, my doctor in Winnipeg had to constantly send in additional paperwork, and I had to let the insurance company know how I was progressing.

I don't know where I would be today without the support of my psychiatrist. If he hadn't been there for me at that time in my life, most likely I wouldn't have taken a leave from work or taken the time I needed to get well. It was a pivotal moment that helped me live a normal, balanced, and successful life, but despite all that, the road ahead was still fraught with danger.

CHAPTER 29

Medications and Excellent Ideas

My anxiety worsened. It was detrimental and crippling and took a toll on my life. All I could do was lie in bed. I couldn't go out, and my body and brain wouldn't allow me to do anything. I tried going for walks, but the anxiety took over my mind.

On June 19, I journaled: "I don't know what to do. I can't get rid of my anxiety. It is so bad. It's in my legs. My brain is overworked. Somebody help me."

I tried Mirtazapine, an antidepressant that wasn't supposed to make you manic, which a lot of anti-depressants can. Two nights after I started that medication, I sat straight up in bed at 2:00 a.m. with my eyes wide open. I was scared I was going to get manic. I became too afraid to take Mirtazapine, and was instead given the antipsychotic medication Abilify. That's when I again got akathisia, and ended up going for walks at least four times a day. Eventually I was put on Lithium.

Three and half months into my leave, I developed depression. Until then, I had hardly had depression in my life. I had to push myself every day to get going. My psychiatrist wrote in his chart: "Appears sad, tearing and feels defeated. Says, 'I am ashamed of my life. I'm ashamed to see people in my family because I'm not working. I should be back at work. I should be able to go back to work. I can't do anything. I can't go out anywhere, can't drive anywhere. Can't make plans to be with friends because I don't know how I'll feel that day.'" He also gave me a workbook called *Mind Over Mood* that contained lots of different exercises I could do to help me feel better. But I thought *really?* Did you not hear what I just said and now you're giving me a book? How is that going to help? However, the workbook helped me look at my situation in a different light and was the beginning of making adjustments to the way I thought so I could feel better.

It still makes me sad to know that my anxiety—and my depression by default—was the likely result of that rotten jail cell in the L.A. County jail system. Even though I have moved on from that dreadful experience, I will never forgive that guard for inflicting pain on my soul by asking me to expose myself.

By August, my anxiety and depression began to worsen. I was struggling with both the lingering pain from jail and my mom's situation. Even though she had finished her treatments, I was still worried about her, and all the while, she was doing what she could to help me. As well as seeing a psychiatrist in Winnipeg, Mom suggested I see a therapist for additional talk time. I decided to contact the Employee Assistance Program that I could access through work. That program helps with problems impacting an employee's home and/or work life. I found out they offered six free counselling sessions, and based on my needs, they connected me with Rose.

Rose had shoulder-length dark brown hair and beautiful blue eyes. Her office was small and had old carpeting. We often talked about my return to work and how afraid I was of what people would say and think. Rose empathized with me and told me to tell people that the reason for my leave was "family issues." When I finally did go back to my job, that worked like a charm. Only one person, an assistant store manager named Shawn, ever asked, "Why were you off work?" When I told him, he simply said, "Oh yeah. Family issues. I know about those."

Rose also suggested baking as an activity. Because of my low energy, I could only function a couple of hours a day, and needed something to do to help me take my mind off the anxiety. Her suggestion proved to be very therapeutic and helped my mind and my soul.

With Rose's encouragement, I started baking after one of Mom's nurse friends introduced me to the website "Sally's Baking Addiction." She and her daughter had made lots of recipes from there, and suggested I give it a try.

Because I love cupcakes, I started with those—a chocolate chip cupcake topped with cookie dough frosting, and a brown sugar butterscotch cupcake. For that second one, I had to make the butterscotch sauce, use an icing decorator to inject the sauce into each cupcake, top them with vanilla frosting, and drizzle with more butterscotch. The last cupcake recipe I made combined a vanilla cupcake with vanilla frosting—my favourite. Each recipe took about two and a half hours to make, which was much better than the four hours it took to make the delicious but time-consuming cheesy breadsticks.

Mom helped out a bit, but I mostly baked alone and made cupcakes for other people—Rose, a neighbour, Tatiana, and my family. Everyone who tried them loved them, which made me very happy. Despite all the joy baking brought me, four months into my leave my soul was still broken. I journaled: "I'm scared to go back to Calgary. What am I scared of? Being alone and scared of anxiety. What is my problem? Why can't I be independent? I need to learn to fend for myself. I know how to do my job well and everything. I have a nice condo and a company vehicle. I'm scared of what everyone is going to think when I go back. What my customers are going to think, what co-workers are going to say to me. What my boss is going to say to me, what grocery managers are going to say to me, what everybody is going to think. I'm terrified to go back. I feel like I can't make it there. I can start in acting, get into stunts and go to Banff. My heart is broken that I can't make it there. Please, "Never be bullied into silence. Never allow yourself to be made a victim. Accept no one's definition of life; define yourself."—Harvey Fierstein.

During one of our sessions, Rose gave me some excellent advice, although I didn't know it at the time. She told me about the bipolar group activities at the Mood Disorders Association of Manitoba in Winnipeg. She explained that anyone could attend—family members, friends—and that people didn't have to be bipolar to attend. "Are you interested?"

"No."

She asked a few more times, and I always said no.

One day, Rose asked, "Why not?"

I looked her in the eyes. "I don't want to be associated with the illness." The words tripped out of my mouth and she never asked me about group again.

In September, my psychiatrist tried to get me into a program at the hospital to help with my self-esteem. Unfortunately, there wouldn't be enough time to do the program because I had to be back at work by the beginning of November. Instead, I started taking the medication Latuda for bipolar depression.

Hot Yoga

Toward the end of September, I volunteered once again at the bakery where I did nutritional work before moving to Calgary. My psychiatrist told me volunteering would improve my self-esteem and reconnect me with work. He was right. The bakery helped me talk to people in a work-like setting, and volunteering made my transition back to work much easier.

The lovely people who owned the bakery knew about my illness, but didn't tell any of their staff. Instead, they did their best to gently encourage me, "Get out and do something. You can't continue to lie on the couch." One suggestion they made was yoga, and they talked to me about it more than once. I mulled their suggestion over for a week and then pushed myself with all my strength to go to hot yoga. Being on mentally ill sick leave made me feel disjointed from the daily activities of life, so doing yoga was both a great accomplishment and helped my mind, body, and soul.

Return to Work

Toward the end of October, the Latuda had started to help with my depression. My psychiatrist told me that while I could go back to work, I should start part-time with a gradual progression to full-time. My parents helped pack up my belongings—my suitcase and backpack filled with clothes, shoes, toiletries, and a couple of pictures—and drove me from Winnipeg to Calgary.

That my parents continue to support me is still amazing to me. Even though my mom was tired for a long time after all that radiation and often had to nap to regain her strength, she didn't let it, or pretty much anything, get her down. Anyone looking in from the outside wouldn't even know she had been through anything. And my dad was a constant source of strength for us both. I don't know where I would be without them.

I started back at work in November 2014. Despite the fact I was welcomed back without question and a lot of my customers were happy to see me, it wasn't easy at first. The job caused some distress and required all my strength and endurance, especially since for much of the previous few months, I spent eighteen hours a day in bed. Initially I worked part-time with the individual who managed my territory when I was on leave.

In late November, I had lunch with my boss. I told him if I could increase my sales numbers from a year ago, I could do anything. He replied, "Go for it."

Every day I made sure to push myself. My mind and my body felt taxed all the time, but I was focused on my goals. As a result, I not only managed to increase my sales numbers, but by the end of December 2014, I was once again working full-time.

Boots and a Dress

By the time the New Year was underway, I finally felt settled back in my condo. My life consisted of going to work, coming home, eating dinner, doing a bit more work after dinner, and going to bed.

As part of my job, I visited various stores and filled up their stock of our product. After writing up each shelf order, I talked to the managers to try and increase the order by getting incremental displays into their store—that meant extra displays, so more products than just a regular shelf order. In some cases, the managers had to sign off on the order quantity and dollar amount, and I was given a purchase order that I entered into my computer.

I was often able to get half pallet displays in stores, which took up more space and really helped with sales. In a big-box store, having a half pallet display means you can sell a large volume of your items in a short amount of time. Full pallets are even better, but I'll take a half pallet over none at all.

Every Tuesday I talked and joked with two women, Shawna and Alicia, in the back office of one particular big-box store on my route. I really liked those women, partly because if they saw I was struggling in some way, they would do what they could to help alleviate my sufferings. If a customer had been rude to me or something about work was bothering me, they would listen and empathize and add a twist on the end to make me chuckle. If I was fogged out from my anxiety or sleeping pills, they helped lighten my mood for a few minutes by making me laugh. Shawna always had a funny story about her family or an idea to increase my sales in her store. The window we talked through was tiny, but not so small that they couldn't see my wardrobe covering my entire body and the large jacket I always wore over everything.

One day Shawna announced, "If you want to get more of your cookies into this store, you need to wear a low-cut shirt, a short skirt, and high heels, and speak to the youngest male manager. That's how the confectionary company rep does it. I've seen her."

That made me chuckle even though the thought of it was ludicrous and I assumed they were simply joking with me.

But after mulling their comments over, I decided I desperately wanted another laugh out of those women. I also thought it might be time for me to try and free myself somewhat from the shackles of my dusty past.

The next Tuesday I wore a wardrobe change—a knee-length fitted colourful dress and boots. There was no sign of cleavage and no short skirt, but it did get the reaction I wanted—smiles and laughter. Every week for the next two months, they insisted that I open their office door and model my outfit for them. They made me feel so good about dressing up, and I felt better about myself. After that, dressing up was a regular occurrence for me. My self-image was no longer hidden from the experience in that dirty, dingy jail cell.

As soon as dresses became a regular appearance, I subtly flirted and teased men. I used humour and gave back the same language they put out, just like my friend Collin had taught me. After jail and after getting lost in the dust, it took a lot for me to get to that point. When I dressed up and felt better, my self-esteem elevated and my body image skyrocketed. There were still moments when I had body image issues, but it was freeing and liberating to uncover my body and show off my curves. When other male reps asked how I sold so many half pallets, I would joke, "Boots and a dress."

Although 2015 was one of my best years at work, I had no social life. All I did was work, eat, sleep, and take pills. I was in bed by 8:00 p.m. and didn't go out with friends because I was afraid my anxiety would kick in or I'd be too tired to drive home.

At that particular time, I had a total of six pill bottles—300 mg Lithium and 150 mg Lithium (mood stabilizer), Zopiclone (sleeping pill), Latuda (antipsychotic), Diazepam (anti-anxiety), and Synthroid (thyroid); some I took every day, like the sleeping pill, and others only when necessary, like the anti-anxiety pill, but all of them put me in a fog and bogged me down. Despite all that, every morning I'd still get up and go to work.

Fighting against my medication was sometimes the hardest part of my struggles with the illness. Many times, I thought about trying to reduce the number of medications I was on, starting with the anti-anxiety and sleeping pills. I had tried acupuncture treatments before and that had helped me get off the anti-anxiety pills for at least six months, so I knew I could do it if I just had the right person helping me. Unfortunately, finding the right health care practitioner took longer than I hoped.

Stiffness Again

One Saturday afternoon in April 2015, I was so stiff and uncomfortable that I took myself to emergency. Several hours passed before I was able to see a doctor, and by then it had gotten much worse. He tested my wrist and arm for cog-wheeling, and concluded that my antipsychotic medication Latuda was the culprit, even though the 20 mg dosage I was on was the smallest pill available. Then I was injected with some other medication to counteract the stiffness, and less than two hours later, the stiffness subsided a bit.

On Monday I tried to get an appointment with my psychiatrist, but the medical assistant wouldn't give me one, even after I explained what had happened. So I called Darrell and left him a message. It was only through the intervention of my therapist that I got an appointment with that psychiatrist.

When I sat down with both the psychiatrist and my therapist, the psychiatrist checked my arm for cogwheeling. “You’re not stiff,” he brusquely announced.

I think he’s angry at me for using Darrell to get me this appointment.

Instead of saying what I was thinking, I simply replied, “The emergency doctor said I was.”

My psychiatrist made me feel like the stiffness was all in my head, but I knew it wasn’t.

Territory Manager of the Year

All my dedication and countless hours at work paid off. By the end of 2015, I had increased my sales by $250,000 more than my numbers for 2014. I sold a tonne of half pallets of cookies and crackers that year. At a Regional Meeting in February 2016, I won Territory Manager of the Year for Western Canada for 2015. And I had done all that without any of my co-workers knowing what I had been through to get there. *I was #1 in sales.*

A month after I received my sales award I had my usual appointment with the psychiatrist. As part of our session, he renewed my prescription, and then we talked about how things were going. When he asked about work, I told him about my award. He looked at me through his glasses and commented, “You know, I can’t compare you to others with bipolar because everybody is different, but from what you’ve been through and the way you are motivated, I think you are remarkable.” A compliment like that from someone who had never given me a compliment before was an incredible feeling. He made my day and helped boost my confidence.

And it was the first time I walked down the hall after a session with a smile on my face.

The Bipolar Group

While I was in Winnipeg on sick leave, Rose had suggested joining a bipolar group; my parents also thought it would be a good idea. I said no because at that time, I didn't want to be associated with the illness. When I moved back to Calgary, my aunt and uncle suggested the same thing, but I still didn't want to be part of that group and I wasn't ready to go anyway. *You can't make somebody do something if they don't want to or they're not ready.* However, I did reluctantly promise them, "If I win sales rep of the year, I'll go to group."

When I received my sales award, I still wasn't sure I wanted to go, but after two more months of trying to get my courage up, I kept my word.

In April 2016, I told my story at a bipolar group.

If it wasn't for Rose's genius idea and my family's persistence and insistence, I would never have gone to that group. And then I would never have experienced the relief that comes from sharing all of my secrets with people who empathize and truly understand. And I would never have listened to *them* and been able to understand what *they* were going through. It was magical beyond belief because I knew there were other individuals like me out there.

At a more recent meeting, someone else commented, "Bipolar is like being in jail. They take away everything from you. Your razor, your clothes, your cell phone, your make-up, your existence, even your clothes—which they replace with ugly coloured hospital pyjamas. You are left with nothing but your manic mind to fend for yourself in ugly light pastel-coloured hospital rooms." I could relate to everything that person said, and I knew I wasn't alone in my struggles anymore.

When individuals with the same illness get together and talk, it is truly a blessing. Most people have no concept of how the mechanics of the brain work when someone is ill. On many occasions, people have said totally wrong and idiotic things to me about mental illness and the individuals who suffer with it. Those people say they are scared or blame those individuals who have it, and that breaks my heart because I know it is not our fault. While there are times when there has been a real reason to be afraid or concerned, I will say again that happens much less than you might think. What we really need is for people to stop and check their general lack of knowledge on the subject before making wildly inaccurate and ill-informed pronouncements about those who are mentally ill. And that would likely require a broader and more targeted and helpful and regular conversation in society about what it is like on the inside to have mental illness. If we can find a way to help people in general to understand and accept what having a mental illness means, then they will be less likely to be afraid and to point fingers and lay blame. Mental illness by itself can give a person enough of a complex. Trust me; we do not need more of a complex because of the unwillingness and ignorance of some members of our society.

And Then He Was Gone

When I wasn't working I had a hard time explaining to people, "I'm off work because I am sick." My brain doesn't function properly when I am mentally ill. I know it's not my fault, but I still feel incompetent and insecure, and lacking in self-esteem. For the rest of my life I will have to explain to anyone with whom I want a relationship that I have bipolar.

At one point in 2015, I began messaging a guy for about six months before we met in person. Even though I didn't want a relationship, we enjoyed going out and having fun. One day he was at my place when he told me a story about being at the gym when the paramedics and police turned up. "There was a person outside yelling and screaming and acting strange," he said. "It was so scary because the person wouldn't calm down, and that terrified me. It was so scary."

That's when I decided to tell him that I have bipolar. His voice went up eight octaves when he spoke. Within two weeks of that conversation he was gone.

Individuals with bipolar have told me that even their partners left them when they were at their worst. It disheartens me that people leave relationships because they can't handle an illness. Emotionally it hurts to know that people run from bipolar.

Walter Winchell once said, "A real friend is one who walks in when the rest of the world walks out," and I believe that to be true. There are people who are genuine, who I love and can talk to, and who I know really care about me, but I still hate telling them that I *was* mentally ill and the medication I am on now keeps me from *being* mentally ill. I hate being pegged as "that mentally insane person" and I hate that every relationship is difficult as a result. I will always have a hard time building new relationships because for a while I was left in the dust and deserted because of my illness, and I am still forced to hide behind it. Fortunately, I don't spend my time worrying about relationships. Instead, I focus on motivating and pushing myself tooth and nail to do well at work every day.

CHAPTER 30

Sleeping Pill Debacle

After my leave of absence in 2014, not working was never again an option for me. I need to work. It keeps me well because it stimulates my mind. My sales achievements in 2015 were significant, and my cost saving efforts helped save the company a lot of money. I was focused on doing even better in 2016.

I made a point of being vigilant about what our competition was doing. I tried to notice whenever new products from other companies hit the shelves, and sometimes, customers would even tell me about another company's products *before* they hit the shelves. Anytime I went to the U.S. I took photos of our competitors' products that weren't already in Canada, and researched what our competitors were doing online so I could be on top of the market and more productive at my job.

In late April, I went to Ontario for two days of training so I could start testing a new computer system. The testing lasted for seven weeks, during which time I also trained other individuals on the system. That required me to work long hours, sometimes eleven to thirteen hours every day, and as a result, I had difficulty sleeping.

In May and June, my sleeping pill nightmare became more of a debacle. The lack of sleep was so bad that at my appointment the psychiatrist increased the dosage not once, but twice. The first time it was increased to one and a half pills (10 mg) and another time to two (15 mg).

Even one sleeping pill made me so exhausted and created such a fog in my life that I didn't always know what was going on. There were times after taking one that I would text or have a phone conversation and not be able to remember anything about it the next day. So the impact of taking *two* pills was ruthless and left my brain so thick with fog that I couldn't think straight or stay focused. I don't know how I survived on that dosage, but somehow my brain found a way to push past the haze and fogginess, and I woke up every morning determined to go to work. After two days of being on 15 mg (two whole sleeping pills), I made the decision to drop the dosage back to the original 7.5 mg.

Unfortunately, because I wasn't sleeping enough, there were no other options but to take at least some dosage of those pills. My psychiatrist reassured me, "You aren't really taking that much," but that was not what I wanted or needed to hear. What I really wanted was to be off the sleeping pills altogether, but it wasn't possible at that time under those circumstances. Instead, I tried to survive, to make it through the day, and to stay as healthy as I could.

A Blank Stare and a Lot of Awkward Pauses

A few weeks later, a job was posted at the company I worked for. The position was in head office working with my favourite big-box customer. I had increased sales with that customer in 2015 by $187,000—that was from selling a lot of extra cookies and crackers. I applied for the position and was thrilled to be given an interview. Since I was attending our national meeting in Muskoka, Ontario, it was decided that I would be interviewed at that event.

During the presentations I received my five-year pin—five years in total with the company. I was also asked to deliver a speech, and to train six other Territory Managers to use the new computer system.

Given the tight schedule at the meeting and the number of other people being considered for the job, my interview was held over breakfast one morning. I didn't really mind that, but in hindsight, it might have been better for me if it was later in the day. I was still struggling from lack of sleep and the effects of the sleeping pill debacle, and because I had to get up at 4:00 a.m. Calgary time two mornings in a row—one to catch a flight, and the other to prepare for the interview—I was extremely tired. Still, I thought the interview went okay, but in fact it didn't go well at all.

The following Tuesday afternoon, I was sitting in my car outside the big-box store where I joked with Shawna and Alicia. When my phone rang, it was the interviewer I had for the job I applied for; he wanted to tell me how the interview went.

The very first thing he said was, "You had a blank stare on your face and a lot of awkward pauses."

Yes, because I was up at 4:00 a.m. two days in a row to make sure I was there and ready for the interview.

His words completely caught me off guard and brought tears to my eyes. Unfortunately, he didn't stop there. "Anyway, I didn't give you the job because I couldn't see you talking to a buyer with that glazed-over look on your face. I'm just helping you in life."

I won sales rep of the year last year. Help me in life? In that moment I felt *ashamed* of my life, ashamed of my illness, and desperate for him not to hear my pain.

The phone call couldn't end fast enough. Tears streamed down my face and snot dripped from my nose. I sat in my car and cried for the next thirty minutes. My dreams of advancing at my job were gone and I was broken.

After that phone conversation I put a screensaver on my work computer that said, "Send me to the wolves and I will return leading the pack." It was a protective mechanism that helped me make an important decision. That interviewer had made me question my illness, but also convinced me that I had to get off the sleeping pills. Although that conversation wounded my heart, it did in fact help me in life.

The Right Health Care Practitioner

By October 2016, I was really struggling. As I wrote in my journal around that time, "I hate my illness. Every day I am reminded of it because of all the pills I take. I used to take one pill and now I take like ten and it hurts so bad. I can't do anything and this illness has ruined my life. It tortures me, it upsets me and I feel like I'll never get out of the position I'm in. It makes me feel like I'm a loser. I have no quality of life. I can't do anything. I'd rather be on one pill and have anxiety than feel the way I feel. I hate my life and am ashamed of my life. I can't live like this anymore."

That was when my pharmacist, Jasmine, helped me get off Diazepam, the anti-anxiety pills I was taking. I went to see her because my body was low in energy and I wasn't feeling well. She was wonderful, always smiling from ear-to-ear, and so intelligent and helpful when explaining medications. When I arrived, I was crying and she took me into a private room and shut the frosted glass door. Then she called up my blood work results on the computer, and after a few minutes, looked at me and said, "You should not be mixing your anti-anxiety pills with your sleeping pills. How often do you take Diazepam?"

"Not every day. Just as needed."

"You should only take those when absolutely necessary."

What I didn't tell Jasmine is for three days *before* that discussion, I was taking anti-anxiety pills every day. After that discussion, however, I stopped taking the Diazepam pills completely. I never looked back, only forward, all because of my pharmacist and her words. Sometimes it just takes the right healthcare practitioner to help change your life for the better.

Writing My Way Back

Finally off the anti-anxiety pills, I started writing about my experience in jail. I had first written about jail in 2011. As I re-wrote, the anxiety came back, but I drew on my taekwondo training to mentally adapt and overcome, and I also wrote my way out of the anxiety. Eventually I didn't need those terrible, numbing pills. The pharmacist had steered me in the right direction, but I cured myself when I wrote about the anxiety and understood where it came from. Although I was off those pills, I was still taking my sleeping pill Zopiclone and every night my body would sink into bed by eight.

Because I had started writing more seriously about my experiences, I was intrigued when I heard about a weekly writing class called "Writing a Memoir When Your Story is Difficult." It ran from 7:00 to 10:00 at night, and given my early-to-bed routine, I thought, *There's no way I can take that class.* But after I read my Aunt Laura and Uncle Doug a piece of my writing, they spent half an hour trying to convince me to sign up for the class. My Uncle Doug commented, "Who cares if you can only take two classes, or only go for one hour and leave? You'll get something out of it." My parents had been telling me for years to write my story, and now with the additional encouragement from my aunt and uncle, I immediately went online and signed up.

My aunt and uncle's encouragement was a turning point for me, as was the recommendation of the female facilitator at the bipolar group. Their combined faith in me helped my book start to take shape—and inspired me to somehow stay up until 10:00 p.m. at least one night every week.

Finally Off the Sleeping Pills

After speaking with Jasmine and writing my way out of anxiety, I decided it was time to do something about my sleeping pill situation. Sometime before my second hospitalization, I didn't sleep for twenty-seven hours in a stretch. Now back home, lack of sleep and mania scared me so much that I had become strict and regimented with respect to the amount of sleep I had, but that had created a vicious cycle. I took Zopiclone to sleep because I was afraid to get ill, and I also took it to cover up the traumatic pain in my life that was the L.A. jail nightmare. Sleeping pills became routine for covering up my anxiety and shutting down the flashbacks of that dirty, dingy cell where I was abused, trapped, and exposed as mentally ill for all the world to see. Everybody there knew I was ill, but instead of helping me, they just screwed with me. The only way I knew how to cover all that up was to put myself to sleep. Breaking that routine would be extremely difficult, but I desperately wanted off those pills and knew nobody else could help me do it. *Nobody can change my life for me; I have to take the first step.*

What scared me most about going off the pills was the possibility that if I didn't sleep I could have another manic episode, be thrown in jail again, and be in a state where my thoughts controlled me and I didn't control them. Still, I made the decision to risk no sleep for just a couple of hours a night.

Weaning myself off the sleeping pills was not easy. I slowly reduced the dosage from 7.5 mg of Zopiclone to 5 mg for about a week, and then 2.5 mg for another week. When I finally stopped taking them altogether, I found myself wide awake for at least two hours every night. I was scared that I'd get ill if I didn't sleep, and I didn't want to go manic. A lot of self-talk was going on in my brain during those early hours. *It's okay if I don't fall asleep right away. The most important thing is to get off the sleeping pills and have a normal functioning life. The sleeping pills don't own me.*

Even though I was a little bit afraid for my life without the pills, I convinced myself I would adapt to the situation and eventually overcome the routine of needing to take a pill to fall asleep. *Sleeping a little less will be far better than a nebulous life.* One pleasant side effect of getting off them was that I dreamt at least twice a week. I never had dreams when I took sleeping pills.

Everything was better without the foggy haze in my life. I excelled at my job, I stayed out later with friends, I attended two groups at night—Mondays in a board room at a hospital, and Wednesdays in a coffee shop—and when I was able to go for a run, I ran easier with a clear head. The second week I was off sleeping pills, I was driving to my writing course and listening to "Amazing" by Aerosmith. There were two lines in the song that took my breath away—the lyrics mentioned something about being all right and the feelings you'll have when that time comes. That was an aha moment for me. I was no longer taking sleeping *or* anti-anxiety pills, and I no longer had that foggy, hazy feeling. I knew I would be all right, and that indeed felt amazing.

Beauty

November 8, 2016, I went on a seven-day vacation to Palm Springs. I had been off sleeping pills for three weeks when I journaled "Beauty":

"I'm back in California. It is the first time since leaving on a jet plane almost six years ago. I feel less beautiful. My blonde hair hangs over my shoulder, my roots are showing and my hair is dry and damaged. My insides feel ugly and I'm not sure why. Beauty is only skin deep but you have to feel beautiful inside to project it outside. After jail my body felt violated, abused, and ugly inside so I covered myself up for years. Returning to California has triggered my memory of that haunting pain. The hatred I have for my body today is because of the flashbacks from jail. I am working on treating my split ends, but my aching self-esteem has been diminished by thoughts of jail—and it hurts so bad. Individuals in the jail played with my emotions and scarred my soul. I have never been the same.

"My mind was at the point of feeling beautiful internally, but the flashbacks from the jail changed that. The chipped paint in that dingy jail cell is like my aching heart, with so many pitted memories. The graffiti is like the marks the jail guards left on my body and the scar on my chin that will never wash away. The formaldehyde my nose smelled reminds me of the stink the guards left on my life. They made me want to hide and to put myself to sleep. Every day there is work to be done to forget my past, to live in the present and to feel beautiful."

I Want to Get into Acting

The next day, I met a Hispanic girl in the hotel restaurant who let me add truffle fries to my meal for only one dollar. She was about five foot seven in heels, wore a silky dress with pink, black and white shapely lines on top and black on the bottom, and looked quite young and innocent. She had dark eyes, dark roots and blonde hair, red lips, and a pretty smile. She told me, "I don't like Palm Springs because of too many older people. I love larger cities where the action is."

"L.A.?" I asked.

"I don't really like L.A. I prefer a beach somewhere." Then she smiled as the words "I want to get into acting" rolled so easily off her tongue.

Those were words I had never been able to say out loud. My passion had always been hidden from everyone. Acting was both my secret passion and my secret world. So many people flock to L.A. to pursue acting, but what I wanted was an outlet or a different form to express the hardships and pain in my life. I wanted to teach the world it was okay to overcome obstacles and share your emotional pain in a scene.

The problem was I didn't want to be an actress *and* have bipolar. I had been off medication for ten years before going to L.A. the first time, so in my mind I wasn't bipolar, but then it resurfaced. The stress my mind went through after I packed up my life and my job and tried to make it work in L.A. had gotten the best of me. The City of Angels swallowed me up whole, chewed me up, and spat me out faster than I could have imagined.

Even then, my dreams of L.A. were only pushed back, not gone, which is why after my illness, I returned to L.A. the second time. That was when my acting teacher had asked, in a round-about way, what had happened to my self-esteem. Sadly I couldn't tell him, "I lost it in my illness."

I know now that bipolar would likely have swallowed me up whole and eaten me for breakfast. The stigma of my illness would have killed my career before it even got started.

CHAPTER 31

No Empathy

On November 12, 2016, after returning from Palm Springs, I had an appointment with my psychiatrist. Most psychiatrists in the city where I currently reside don't do therapy as well. They only handle your medication, while a therapist looks after the therapy portion. That was initially a big adjustment for me because my psychiatrist in Winnipeg had provided therapy *and* discussed medication. So I found sessions in Calgary tremendously difficult because I didn't think the psychiatrist could possibly understand me as a person without also doing some kind of therapy. And because at first I didn't think he had taken the time to study and understand me as a person, I felt like he was always pushing pills on me. One of the greatest gifts a psychiatrist can have is empathy, so when a psychiatrist only writes out prescriptions, his empathy is misplaced.

On the Friday of that week I talked to Darrell about my book and my experience in the L.A. County jail system. He worked in the jail system in Canada, and after listening to my story, simply said, "They did that because of the hierarchy of the system." He explained that the guards abused me and played with me to maintain a position of superiority—by abusing their power, they could move up the ranks and get a better job. Hearing that was hard to take, partly because it reminded me that I was a pawn caught up in a situation over which I had no control, but also because I was hoping for more empathy from this person with whom I had just shared one of the most traumatic experiences in my life.

At the end of the session Darrell walked me to the end of the hospital hall like he always did, and before we parted, he said, “Enjoy the journey you’re on.” That instantly reminded me again of the song “Amazing” by Aerosmith. That song always made me think about my journey, my destination, love, accomplishing goals, and never settling.

In December 2016, I had a session with both the psychiatrist and Darrell. During the session I cried as I talked about the looming layoffs at work, how stressed I was at the possibility of being let go, and how my energy levels had sunk as a result. After listening to my story, the psychiatrist suggested adding an antidepressant to my other medications.

I thought about that, and then said, “Instead of adding anything, I’d actually like to decrease my Lithium.” Twenty years before, Lithium had caused me to sleep eighteen hours a day, and in 2016, I was taking a total of 750 mg a day of that medication—two 300 mg pills and one 150 mg pill.

Judging by the look on my psychiatrist’s face, he didn’t like that idea at all.

When we got onto the topic of anti-anxiety pills, I announced, “I’ve been off them since the beginning of October.”

The psychiatrist gave a half grin. “What about the sleeping pills?”

"I've been off of them since October 22. My neighbour told me she thought I was overmedicated. My friend agreed with my neighbour."

My psychiatrist wasn't grinning anymore. "Your neighbour and your friend saying you were overmedicated is their perception. And 7.5 mg of Zopiclone is *not* overmedicated."

"Yes, but 15 mg of Zopiclone *and* Diazepam is."

Both the psychiatrist and Darrell appeared to be a bit flustered, but it still came as a complete surprise to me when later in the session, they discussed discharging me from therapy. *They think I'm unstable and they still want to kick me out of therapy?* I began to cry and my voice shook as I said, "It will be hard to find a good relationship again like the one I have with you, Darrell." His only response was to reassure me I would find someone else to connect with.

At the end of that session, the psychiatrist again suggested adding an anti-depressant. I countered by reiterating that instead I wanted to decrease the Lithium. He reluctantly agreed to reduce the dosage from 750 mg to 600 mg.

I advocated for myself and on that day my pill bottles went down to three.

Advocating for Myself

During my next session with Darrell, I advocated for myself again. I was direct and told him that while I still wanted to be able to see him, I would rather see a different psychiatrist.

"Where is that coming from?" he asked.

I thought about his question for a moment before replying. "In our bipolar group, we talked about the importance of having a good relationship with our respective psychiatrists, and I don't believe I have that at all."

We then discussed options for changing my situation, but nothing was decided. Instead, Darrell again brought up the topic of discharging me from therapy. I was stunned. *That is not at all what I thought would happen when I advocated for myself.*

Then, in my last session with Darrell, he officially discharged me from therapy. I shouldn't have been all that surprised because technically, people are supposed to only get something like twelve weeks of sessions, and I got a little more than three years. Still, I liked Darrell, and was sorry our time was at an end.

With only a couple of minutes left in my session, Darrell handed me a red book and said, "This is for you." It was called *Wellness Recovery Action Plan* by Mary Ellen Copeland, and was a self-designed prevention and wellness tool for getting well and staying well. Then I filled out a survey where I explained what I needed as part of my therapy—a good relationship with a psychiatrist rather than one who lacks empathy and pushes pills. I was angry when I filled out the form because I knew it would be difficult to find a psychiatrist who was focused more on empathy than pushing pills, and also because I knew I would have to stay with my current psychiatrist while I looked for someone else.

The Grass is Not Always Greener

February 2017, I began shopping for a new psychiatrist. I hoped to find a more balanced patient-psychiatrist relationship like I had in Winnipeg, but I quickly learned that might not be something I would ever find again.

It's very difficult to get a psychiatrist at all in Calgary, and it takes some people a year to find one. The process is different for each person, but some people are forced to take what they get, even if they aren't compatible. The situation is very sad.

Fortunately, I didn't have to wait that long. The new psychiatrist was a pleasant enough East Indian man in a rougher part of town. His dimly lit office was on the second floor of a strip mall behind a grocery store, and instead of a couch or a comfortable chair, there was only a straight-back chair for me to sit on. After only talking to me for about twenty minutes, he concluded, "You are in that small percentage of bipolar individuals that are afraid to go out and live their life." *Excuse me?* He didn't know me from a hole in the wall, and that comment was both surprising and unnerving.

It is true that I am afraid of relationships and afraid to get excited. Relationships have been difficult because ever since that nurse misjudged me back in 1998, I have pushed down my feelings and kept them hidden for fear of being judged by other people. Excitement scared me to the point that I would push it down to the bottom of my stomach in the hope it would go away. When I had manic episodes, my mind and body got so excited that when I was well I was scared to feel excited about *anything*. I don't want to become manic ever again. That is how bipolar debilitates me. Even when I am not suffering with symptoms, the thought of becoming manic still frightens me.

At the end of the session, the psychiatrist told me he wouldn't change my medication at that point, but suggested I consider increasing the dosage of Latuda I was taking from 20 mg to 40 mg, which was the recommended dose for that medication. *Why would anyone suggest changing my pills when I am doing well?* I didn't say anything to him about that, but given my reaction to it back in April 2015, I knew I would not be following his suggestion.

During that very interesting session, I realized that after having a psychiatrist with empathy and who works for you and with you like my psychiatrist in Winnipeg, it is very difficult to find another one who matches up. *The grass is not always greener on the other side.* So when the East Indian man suggested I stay with my current psychiatrist, I decided he was right. I had been with that psychiatrist for a little more than three years, and even though he was very different to the one in Winnipeg, I believed he had helped me.

After all that, shopping for a psychiatrist had complicated my situation and made me feel worse about myself. Despite being discharged by Darrell, I knew I still needed therapy. Self-care is extremely important to my survival, and I decided to try a different professional altogether. I set out to find myself a psychologist.

Psychologist

My first appointment with the psychologist was also in February, shortly after my failed attempt to find a new psychiatrist. For the second time, I was able to find someone to help me through the Employee Assistance Program at work. The fact that sessions were free and confidential was very important to me.

The first thing I noticed when I arrived was how much brighter her office was compared to the East Indian psychiatrist. There was also a beautiful leather couch for me to sit on, while she sat on a chair. Her brown hair was chin length. When I told her I didn't get the job I had applied for at my company, she asked, "How do you feel about that?"

I looked up and to the left as I thought of a response. "I was upset at the time, but I am thankful now because I would have never have been able to finish my book." I explained to her that I would have had to move across the country and probably been overworked at the new position, which meant I wouldn't have had the time or the energy to continue writing my book and working on myself.

"That's a positive way to look at it." She always spoke calmly and softly.

In another session, she asked, "When did you know you wanted to be an actress?"

"When I was first hospitalized at seventeen."

"Why did you want to be an actress?"

"When I took acting classes, I loved performing and I loved being on set. It was magical beyond belief. And I connected with the feelings and emotions acting provoked in me. Every day I knew I would love my job as an actress and be thankful." I paused before adding, "Also, because I thought that having bipolar wouldn't matter. If my moods were up or down, people would just think I was acting and they wouldn't judge."

Coincidently, that same week I was at a learning group talking about the occupations of bipolar individuals. A guy in the group said that a lot of artists, writers, and poets are more productive when they are manic, and that "bipolar individuals often choose occupations that have more allowance for their personality."

WHAM. That hit me like a lightning bolt. "Can you say that again please?"

He looked at me through his glasses. "Bipolar individuals often choose occupations that have more allowance for their personality."

I wrote that down immediately. My whole life I had been searching for an occupation that allowed my creative juices to flow, and at the same time allowed my personality—bipolar or not—to shine through. And that was why my mind, body, and soul wanted to act—for the simple reason of allowing my personality to shine.

Stiffness Prevailed

Everything was going well for me. Work was busy and stable, and I felt happy. But then something quite unexpected happened.

During an appointment with my psychiatrist on Friday October 27, 2017, he noticed that I appeared to be suffering from some stiffness. Although he immediately recognized it as a side-effect of the antipsychotic medication Latuda, he didn't know what to do at first because he had only ever seen that when a patient started a medication, not three years after the fact. I told him that was part of the reason I was diagnosed as "atypical," and that if it continued to get worse, I would be in emergency that weekend.

By Saturday the awful stiffness had taken over my entire body, and as I predicted, I ended up in emergency. They couldn't administer Cogentin because that medication had previously caused severe blurred vision, so instead they gave me Benadryl. For a brief moment, I flashed back to the first time I was on a psych ward and they also gave me needles in the rear end. This time, however, I wasn't fighting against the injection.

At the beginning of November I was completely taken off Latuda, which meant I was only on two medications—Lithium and Synthroid. And the only reason I was taking the thyroid medication Synthroid was because the Lithium had knocked my thyroid out of whack. As I said before, dealing with my medication was sometimes the hardest part of my struggles with the illness.

Self-Care

Six days later, I was rear-ended in a car accident just like in 1996 before my first manic episode. That was not the stressor I needed in my life after discontinuing a medication, but I survived because I made sure to take care of myself. If I have learned anything from this entire journey it is that self-care is the most important thing for individuals with bipolar.

If you have bipolar, self-care is essential for maintaining wellness. Indeed, it is now one of the main priorities in my life. Whatever my body needs, within reason, I make sure my body gets—plenty of sleep, taking a relaxing bubble bath, running and exercising, colouring, meditating, getting a massage, going for acupuncture, and wearing my favourite perfume. For me, particular perfume scents trigger feelings from favourite memories that calm my soul. I used to save my perfumes for special occasions, such as going out at night, but now I use them any time, even if it's just to do errands or go for a run.

It also helps me to listen to soft music, including my favourite Aerosmith ballads—"Cryin'," "Amazing," and "Crazy"—and to watch favourite television shows. *Three's Company*, for example, was always on the television in my house as a child, either as re-runs or when I watched episodes I had recorded on VHS tapes. That show provided me with many days of rest and relaxation, particularly during university. The laugh track soothed my soul, and I had memorized almost every episode. That show was one of my all-time favourites because John Ritter was so funny.

Living in the present is also good for me, and part of that involves not saving things all the time like I used to—perfumes, clothes, shoes, and purses.

CHAPTER 32

Return to Los Angeles

After getting me out of jail and safely back to Winnipeg in January 2011, my mom had told me, "I don't ever want to go to L.A. again." My arrest and the treatment of me in the jail system had been very traumatic for her. So it was a huge surprise when she and my dad agreed to fly into L.A. and attend a Jewel concert with me. When I asked her why, Mom told me she had seen how much writing my story had improved my life and how hard I was working to take care of myself. She wanted to go with me so she could share in that special moment.

Our first day in L.A., she and I got the stomach flu, but neither one of us threw-up. The second day we still weren't feeling well, but decided to drive to an outlet mall. On the way there, we passed the exit sign Alameda. Alameda is the street address of the jail where I was told I would die. I immediately felt nauseous in the pit of my stomach. The next morning I was researching L.A. jails online for my book when I felt sick. As soon I walked into the washroom, I threw-up in the tub. Some might say it was the flu, but I honestly believe it was because of that sign, which brought back all the gut-wrenching memories from my time in the L.A. County jail system. It was the only time I threw up in L.A., and it was right when I was thinking about all the unfortunate mentally ill people who had been through and were still stuck in that system.

The next day we drove to Santa Ynez, California, and on December 1, 2017, we saw Jewel. I had dreamed of that moment ever since connecting with her music when I was hospitalized at age seventeen. During the concert when Jewel introduced her song about the hardships and anxiety she had when she was eighteen, tears began to slowly roll down my cheek. I truly believed this person, whose music had been so instrumental in my life, understood a small part of what I had gone through. And in that moment, Jewel touched my soul.

Narrative Therapy

I only went to three sessions with the psychologist because she made me talk the entire time. I prefer it when the person I see asks more questions. Because it wasn't the type of therapy I felt comfortable with, I contacted my therapist Rose in Winnipeg. When I explained the situation and what I was looking for, she recommended a narrative therapist in Calgary.

Narrative therapy holds that people themselves are not the problem, but they are under the influence of the problem that affects their lives and relationships. That way of thinking struck a chord with me and I knew it was something I was willing to try. And all because of Rose. She turned out to be one of the most amazing individuals in my journey so far.

I first went to my narrative therapist in May 2017. She was empathetic, a wonderful listener, and always asked lots of questions to keep me engaged. When I talked to her about throwing up after I saw the Alameda sign, she asked, "What other things can you connect with when you see the "jail" sign now in your mind?"

As I talked, she wrote, and together we came up with a list:

- I lived to tell about it (I didn't die in Alameda, as others predicted)
- I'm way stronger since surviving the experience
- Things don't bother me how they used to
- I'm playing a part for holding others responsible for abusive practices
- I've lived the life of an eighty-year-old after what I've been through
- The things I've experienced and seen, others don't see in a lifetime

For each item, she asked, "How does that make you feel?" or "What is that like?" I was very comfortable telling her because I knew she was trying to help me, and wasn't looking to judge me.

Putting together that list helped me see everything I had gone through, and understand how it makes me feel. I've definitely been through a lot, but I am still here to talk about it. Most things in life don't bother me as much as they used to. And even though most people won't ever see what I've seen in my lifetime, I want everyone to know that I've struggled a lot and I'm still here.

Rainbows and Butterflies

I love quotes and recently downloaded an app that provides me with a new quote every day. The first one that popped up after downloading the app was by German writer and statesman Johann Wolfgang von Goethe: "Whatever you can do, or dream you can do, begin it. Boldness has genius, power and magic in it." It is a quote that goes well with my personality because I truly believe that if you begin your dream and are bold, there will be magic in what you achieve.

Which brings me to the question some of you might want to ask me: "Why aren't you pursuing acting or stunt work?"

That question is not easy to answer, so let me just say this: After my time in jail, after my struggles, and after the trauma I experienced, my life was not full of rainbows and butterflies. Instead, I hid from people I loved and who loved me because I couldn't tell them where I had been or what I had gone through. I was afraid they would think I was a bad person because I disappeared, but the reality was I couldn't face the truth of my own illness. It hurt my heart so much that I *had* to hide. Every day when I take a pill to help the mechanics of my brain, I am reminded of my illness, but for a while, the stigma of that illness haunted me and caused me to suffer, to push it down, to try and lock it away.

But then it would build up in my heart and block me from connecting with people I loved or confronting people who had hurt me, and that made me feel worse. I knew I had so much to offer the world and wanted the opportunity to show people everything I could do. I hoped and prayed that my illness didn't stop me from being the best I could be.

My taekwondo instructor used to say that if one door closes, kick another one open. But my foot had to reach out too far to kick open another door because of all the hurt in my heart. Opportunities were not easily available with my suffering and time off from work on my resume. Eventually, however, I listened to my taekwondo instructor's words about kicking doors open, and to my psychiatrist's words about accepting limitations is part of growing up, to the words of other individuals with bipolar, and to the sage advice of so many people on my journey. I listened and let their words help me adapt my mind to what I suffered with and to overcome obstacles. Their words put me on a path for success.

One day in group, I heard the parents of a bipolar patient say, "Maybe if our daughter was a better person." Being a better person is something I have struggled with my whole life, and I know it isn't as easy as that. I often thought if I could have been a better person then maybe bipolar would have never happened to me, but that is simply not true. Bipolar is the result of the chemicals in my brain, and has nothing to do with being a better person.

The only way to understand the pain and suffering of anyone with bipolar is to listen to what they themselves say about their mental illness. Musician Alfred Brendel once said, "The word 'listen' contains the same letters as the word 'silent.'" So instead of judging, stop and think for a minute before you say something without empathy about someone with mental illness. Silence really is a virtue.

Sometimes I still dream about being an actress and doing stunt work, but I know that is not the pathway I am on right now. Instead, I wake up every day with different goals inspired by the life I am living now. I push myself to achieve those goals because nobody else can. I will never again let my illness take over what I want to accomplish. And I will never again hide myself away from those I love and who love me. My sense of humour and my new understanding of who I am work together to carry me through each day. I believe that eventually my boldness will show the world my capabilities. And I believe this book is the first step in doing exactly that.

My goal in writing this book is to help alleviate the stigma of mental illness. But in order to do that, I needed to first write this book for myself. So I indulged in my own story, ripped out all the heart ache, improved my health, put my tears on the page, and made myself feel better. I knew if I helped myself, I could help others. I want to be a positive role model, and if my memoir can help one person, it is one more person than before.

Entrepreneur and businessman Steve Jobs once said, "You can't connect the dots looking forward; you can only connect them looking backward. So you have to trust that the dots will connect in the future." I was only able to connect the dots after I looked back and began writing my story. In doing so I helped myself, and that was the greatest gift. I trust that the dots will align in the future, and that when they do, I will feel magical and powerful, my life will be full of rainbows and butterflies.

EPILOGUE

I have trained to be a mentor and helped facilitate a group at bipolar meetings. It is rewarding to help other people.

At one bipolar meeting we talked about how psychiatrists seem to be good if they understand the "art" behind it. Some of the people were saying there is a science and an art to psychiatry.

My narrative therapist helped me work through my L.A. County Jail pain and was a really good fit.

My life has changed tremendously since I wrote this book but I couldn't include everything.

L.A. County's Men's Central Jail will be getting an inmate treatment center worth $2.2 billion (2018). Hopefully they will train jail staff to treat mentally ill people with dignity and respect.

I hope this inspires individuals to write their story.

Thank you to my editor Jenny who's word and questions provoked something inside of me and helped shape and define my memoir. Also, thank you to my parents for always being there for me and encouraging me to write my book. The support you have given me is the reason I am where I am today. You always look out for me in the best possible way. Thank you Michael for being the best brother a sister could ask for and an extraordinary role model in sports, music and school. Thank you to my psychiatrist in Winnipeg who was always there for me at any twist or bend in the road. Your patience, compassion and empathetic nature are incredible. You should teach other psychiatrists how to be remarkable psychiatrists. Thank you to my aunt and uncle who helped my parents in the L.A. County jail system when they needed 'stability' the most. Also, thanks for pushing me to take the course 'Writing a Memoir When Your Story is Difficult' and always looking out for me and helping me when my life is difficult. Thanks Karen for teaching a great course. To all my friends, thank you for being there, helping me through tough times and never leaving me when my mind turned me against you. You add sunshine to my life and brighten my days.

REFERENCES

American Psychiatric Association. 1980. *Diagnostic and Statistical Manual of Mental*

Disorders, Third Edition. Arlington, VA. [revised 1987]

American Psychiatric Association. 1994. *Diagnostic and Statistical Manual of Mental*

Disorders, Fourth Edition. Arlington, VA. [revised 2000]

American Psychiatric Association. 2013. *Diagnostic and Statistical Manual of Mental*

Disorders, Fifth Edition. Arlington, VA.

Balsamo, M. 2017. "Spike in mentally ill LA jail inmates leads to new policies."

https://www.usnews.com/news/best-states/california/articles/2017-04-29/la-jail-adapts-amid-meth-fueled-rise-in-mentally-ill-inmat

Battaglia, S. 2004. *The Complete Guide to Aromatherapy*. Zillmere: Perfect Potion.

County of Los Angeles, California (n.d.) *Treatment and Transformation*. [Fact Sheet] retrieved from http://www.cctfproject.org

Frost, Julie A. 2015. "What is the difference between bipolar disorder and schizo-affective disorder?" *bp Magazine*. https://www.bphope.com/blog/what-is-the-difference-bw-bipolar-disorder-and-schizo-affective-disorder/

Dixon, Hayley. 2013. "Controversial acne drug blamed for a number of suicides."

http://www.telegraph.co.uk/news/health/10160484/Controversial-acne-drug-blamed-for-a-number-of-suicides.html

Hare, B. and Rose, L. 2016. "Pop. 17, 049: Welcome to America's largest jail." *CNN*.

http://www.cnn.com/2016/09/22/us/lisa-ling-this-is-life-la-county-jail-by-the-numbers/index.html [Includes video introduction to an episode titled "Inside L.A. County Jail" on Lisa Ling's CNN program "This is Life"]

Hoffmann-La Roche Ltd. 1988. *Important information about your treatment with Accutane* [pamphlet].

Hoffmann-La Roche Ltd. 2014. *Accutane Roche: Part III: Consumer Information*.
Mississauga, ON.

Marcellino, Elizabeth. 2018. "LA County's 'decrepit' Men's Central Jail will be replaced by

$2.2 billion inmate treatment center." *Daily News*. http://dailynews.com/2018/06/19/la-countys-decrepit-mens-central-jail-will-be-replaced-by-2-2-billion-inmate-treatment-center/

The National Institute of Mental Health. 2018. "Bipolar Disorder." Retrieved from

http://nimh.nih.gov/health/topics/bipolar-disorder/index.shtml

Thomson Reuters. 2017. "California Code, Penal Code – PEN 851.5." Retrieved from

http://codes.findlaw.com/ca/penal-code/pen-sect-851-5.html

Thomson Reuters. 2017. "California Code, Welfare and Institutions Code – WIC 5150."

Retrieved from http://codes.findlaw.com/ca/welfare-and-institutions-code/wic-sect-5150.html

Urban Dictionary. (2011). "Hollywood." (DampHair, February 27, 2011).
https://www.urbandictionary.com

Urban Dictionary. (2011). "Tray." (Cassandra Q, October 29, 2011)
https://www.urbandictionary.com

Printed in Canada